Beating
The
Odds

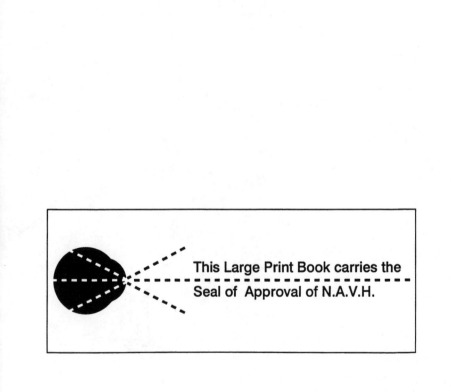

This Large Print Book carries the
Seal of Approval of N.A.V.H.

BEATING THE ODDS

Stories of Unexpected Achievers

Janet Bode

Drawings by Stan Mack

Thorndike Press • Thorndike, Maine

Library of Congress Cataloging in Publication Data:

Bode, Janet.
  Beating the odds : stories of unexpected achievers /
by Janet Bode ; drawings by Stan Mack.
    p. cm.
    ISBN 1-56054-591-7 (alk. paper : lg. print)
    1. Success in adolescence—Case studies. 2. Self-
actualization (Psychology) in adolescence—Case studies.
3. Self-perception in adolescence—Case studies. 4. Large
type books. [1. Success. 2. Self-actualization
(Psychology) 3. Self-perception. 4. Large type books.]
I. Title.
[BF724.3.S9B63   1993]   92-33871
305.23'5—dc20   CIP

Thorndike Large Print® Teen Scene Series edition
published in 1993 by arrangement with Franklin
Watts, Inc.

Cover design by Studio 3.

The tree indicium is a trademark of Thorndike Press.

This book is printed on acid-free, high opacity paper. ∞

To
Margaret Bode

CONTENTS

ACKNOWLEDGMENTS

This book would not have been possible without the support of my family and friends. Special praise goes to:

My father and fellow writer, Carl Bode; my stepmother, Charlotte; and my sisters, Barbara and Carolyn.

My partner, Stan Mack.

My friends Wendy Caplin, Lucy Cefalu, Jeanne Dougherty, Andrea Eagan, Ted Gottfried, Ernie Lutze, Frieda Lutze, Ken Mack, Pearl Mack, Peter Mack, Carole Mayedo, Marvin Mazor, Rosemarie Mazor, Mike Sexton.

I received invaluable assistance from these other sources:

In New York, N.Y.:
Bob Billenger and Joyce Ku, New Amsterdam Library; Elizabeth Long, Lincoln Center Library; Victoria Polk, Satellite Academy High

School; Reva Spero, school social worker.

Donna Chumas, librarian, Patchogue-Medford High School, Medford, N.Y.

Winifred Duncan, city of Chicago School District 299; Mary Jo Neville, media specialist, Curie High School, Chicago, Ill.

In Greensboro, N.C.:
Sylvia Meisner, media specialist, Allen Middle School; Robberta Mesenbrink, assistant principal, Smith High School; Brucie Shook, media specialist, Mendenhall High School; Mary Tedder, media specialist, Lincoln High School.

Marty Podskoch, Delaware Academy and Central School, Delhi, N.Y.

In Los Angeles, CA.:
Nancy Reich, coordinating librarian, Library Services, Los Angeles Unified School District; Momoyo Tada, library media teacher, Garfield High School; Juanita Walker, library media teacher, Crenshaw High School.

Livia Rosenbaum, librarian, Midwood High School at Brooklyn College, Brooklyn, N.Y. Nel Ward, media center director, Maryvale

High School, Phoenix, AZ.

And special thanks to Iris Rosoff, Franklin Watts, Inc.

1
WHAT THIS BOOK IS ABOUT

Nearly seven million children ages ten to seventeen are considered "at risk" of becoming troubled, unproductive, even dangerous adults.[1]

Do you know anyone like this? If so, this book is for you.

The first time I meet Keisha, I think to myself, "What an amazing person." You name it, she's doing it: honor student, peer counselor, pep squad member, budding writer. She radiates enthusiasm and confidence.

The one thing she doesn't like to talk about is where she is living. For Keisha, her four brothers, and her mother, home is a welfare hotel. The six of them squeeze into two rooms already inhabited by more cockroaches than Keisha cares to count.

Poverty is something she's known all her life.

"Why doesn't she feel defeated by poverty?" I wonder. "Does she have a secret recipe for success?" And, if she's beating the odds against her, others must be, too. I decide to investigate.

I will go looking for today's teenagers to talk to those trying to succeed despite serious problems in their lives. I'll consult adult experts, also. What do they have to say on this subject?

My goal is to provide advice to those in trouble who want to change, but don't quite know how or where to start, by showing how other teenagers help themselves.

I visit junior and senior high schools, in New York City, in Los Angeles, and in cities in between. I talk with groups of students. "Are you overcoming difficulties in your own lives?" I ask. Some volunteer to talk with me further.

I call librarians for help. I go after other leads as I come up with more names. My list grows.

When I make arrangements to interview these teenagers, I have no idea what stories will unfold. I only know I'm hearing from young people of different ethnic, economic, and geographic backgrounds. I feel as if I'm going on an adventure.

At an agreed-upon time, two of us meet,

sometimes in person, sometimes over the phone. We discuss the idea behind the book. They know this is serious business. They and I hope that you, the reader, will learn from their experiences.

"To protect your privacy, I'll change your name and other details that might give away your identity," I tell these teens. A few don't care. Most want that guarantee. These are painful secrets they share.

I tape-record the conversations and take notes. (Machines and I aren't always in sync.) As we talk for the next couple of hours, I listen for the "burn" in their voice, the intensity. That is my sign, the story I follow.

And what I hear are tales of tragedy and triumph. They speak of a mother's suicide, of beatings, unplanned pregnancy, physical disability, drugs, alcoholism, murder, a forced marriage at fifteen. . . .

Sometimes the grammar isn't perfect. The verb tenses shift back and forth. But, I believe, the spirit behind the words remains absolutely clear.

The events and the emotions are real. The message gets through. These kids are all struggling, some against almost insurmountable odds.

After I talk to the teenagers, I ask different adults the same basic questions: What are your personal rules for success? What works for you that might work for others?

The answers are as varied as the people I turn to. A child psychiatrist says that you must have a sense of your future.

A personality-research psychologist with an international reputation explains the connection between controlling cookie-eating and success.

A neighbor local kids rely on for sane advice and understanding discusses "quiet time."

A mayor of a major city, an optimism expert, and a probation officer add their thoughts, too.

You won't find "Ten Easy Steps to Change Your Life and Become a Success!!" in this book. The world's not that simple. In fact, there are things about yourself you can't change: your height or your original set of parents, for instance.

But you can improve your attitude, strengthen your belief in yourself, and change your future.

In these pages you will find examples of teenagers trying different roads to a better life. They don't tiptoe around their problems. They tell them straight. They show how they conquered their fears and changed what could be changed.

These kids are the ones who decide they want not just to survive, but to thrive. "Succeed," "Be somebody," "Make it," "Help others" are some of the words they use to describe this desire.

Read through their stories. Check out the information from the adults, too. It doesn't matter which chapter you start with. What matters is that the words you do read offer clear, concise help. What worked for others may work for you.

SOURCE

1. *"Help for At-Risk Kids," Time,* 26 June 1989; "Turning Points: Preparing American Youth for the 21st Century." Report sponsored by Carnegie Corporation of New York.

2
KEISHA, 16, A SOPHOMORE

PART I

I was twelve when we were evicted. My mother stretched the money she earned, but this time the pressure was on. Me and my four brothers were getting older. We needed more things. So she got behind in the rent for an apartment filled with rats and roaches.

After that, it was welfare. They moved us into a shelter. It was terrible!

Hundreds of people were pushed into five floors. We lived on the floor that was like a cafeteria. A bunch of beds in one room. No privacy. Everybody could see you. Kids were running around, fighting and worse.

My mother told us straight out, "Look. I really love you guys. I'm not going to lie. I only have this amount of money. If you need anything, come to me. Don't steal. Don't get yourselves in trouble."

And we listened. We stayed together. As

a family, instead of getting weaker, we got stronger.

I was *always* strong and sure of myself. I *never* hesitated. Interesting, huh? Even my first-grade teacher, Irma Marian, would say, "Keisha, I admire you. You have self-esteem."

I was, like, "Self what?"

She wrote it on the board and said, "When you believe in yourself, you have self-esteem." She knew I was the kind of person who *wants* to make it. When all the shelter noise kept me from sleeping at night, I said to myself, "I'll be okay. I'm a determined person."

Six months later, we had to leave that shelter. There was a time limit. Next, welfare sent us to a hotel shelter, the Imperial. For us, it was a move up. We were happy. We had two rooms of our own and a bathroom. No kitchen.

My mother — like everybody else in the hotel — bought a hot plate to cook her wonderful vegetable pie. A hot plate was illegal, but there were so many things going on, no one said anything.

You see, people did drugs, drugs, drugs. In the hallways. In their rooms. Out front. You had to choose whether or not you wanted to be with that crowd.

People posed as everything, too. They had

keys to each room. You wondered, is the man coming to fix the leak in the bathroom who he says he is?

My mother never left the room unguarded. She didn't want what little we had to be stolen.

Still, the only thing that scared me were the guns. They could go off any time.

One afternoon I'm coming out of a store. This guy pulls up in a red car. Right there in front of me, *blam, blam, blam,* and my thirteen-year-old friend, Antron, is shot, dead.

I wasn't scared to have drugs in front of me, though. I knew I would say no. I wasn't scared of the security guards; they had no reason to touch me. I wasn't scared of the other people in the hotel. I kept to myself.

At the same time, my mother encouraged us and disciplined us. We were too busy to get in trouble.

My brothers were either at school, playing ball, or at work. They packed bags at the grocery store, washed cars, delivered pizza — anything to get a little money.

I decided I wanted to be a writer. My mother said, great, but don't forget first to do my chores. We had to take the garbage out, make the beds, do the dishes, mop, sew. She told my brothers, "Just because you're boys doesn't cripple you from doing these things, too."

She wanted to make sure that all her kids were "glued together." Every day she sent us to school together to make sure we went and came back safely.

At school, some boy pointed to a student named Randall and said, "Oh, he lives in the Hotel Imperial." Everybody laughed. I could tell he felt bad.

After class I went up to him and said, "Do you live in the Imperial?"

"Yeah," he said, "do you want to laugh at me, too?"

"No, no. I'm your neighbor!" That same day we went home together and just became buddy-buddy. We cheered each other up. We went to the park on Saturdays. The museum. The laundromat.

A lot of the other kids at the hotel made fun of us 'cause we didn't use drugs and wanted to make it in school. They called us wannabe whites.

PART II

I never want to be like everyone else, anyway. I don't want to say, "Oh, my friend Janeen is using drugs; I'll use drugs, too." I want to be *better* than Janeen.

If I have to do bad things to be in the *in*

crowd, forget it. I won't do those things to get someone to like me. What I do instead is find people who like me for who I am.

Part of life is that you *have* to make decisions. You can't just sit back and let life happen to you. Also, it's the person who makes the difference, not where you live.

I go to school with pride.

Once there, the students and teachers just keep me going. There are Puerto Ricans, Dominicans, Chinese, whites, blacks. I mix with everyone.

I watch how people deal with different situations. When you do that, you find all kinds of ideas for how to do things. You grow wiser.

Now don't get me wrong. I'm definitely proud that I'm black. You *should* follow your heritage, your culture. But forget about that, "I'm an African-American. I'm only going to associate with my people, because white people did this and this to us."

The more people you meet, the better. Extend your friendship to everyone. By ninth grade, I knew the whole school.

When it comes to romance, though, I do scare boys. If they want to say something, I get into this whole conversation. They're, like, "Oh, she talks too much." I think they're looking for someone just to listen.

Every time I hear a guy put down a girl,

I say, "Why do you talk about girls like that?"

This gets the boys mad. They complain, "Keisha thinks she's smarter than us."

One guy says, "I can get any girl into a bedroom."

"Women are not going to take that talk anymore," I tell him.

"You nerd."

"I may be a nerd," I say, "but I'll never let any man dominate me."

"Why do you use all those big words? You think you're somebody?"

"Yeah, I *am* somebody!" I say.

He makes me laugh. When I *do* become somebody, he'll be saying, "I remember her from school. . . ."

PART III

One day I was walking down the street a few blocks from the Imperial and came to the office of a weekly newspaper. I went inside.

I saw this woman and told her, "I want to be a writer." At first she didn't really listen to me. I guess she thought I was crazy.

She was, like, "Yeah, that's good."

I tugged on her again. I said, "This is a newspaper. I want to write and make money and be a star reporter."

She said, "This is a joke, right?"

"I'm serious," I told her.

"Look, sweetheart," she said, "how old are you?"

"I'm thirteen."

"Where do you live?"

"Down the street."

"At the Hotel Imperial?"

I was embarrassed to have people know I lived there, but I said, "Yes."

"Well, we're starting a program for homeless kids."

"I'm not homeless," I said. "I just live in temporary housing."

After she told me I had a smart mouth, she said the newspaper and some neighborhood people were starting a program to take back a park from drug dealers. They would teach me to help round up little kids, go to the park, and counsel them about drugs, sexual assault, that kind of thing.

"But does that have anything to do with writing?"

"We might do some articles about it," she said.

"I'll be there."

I loved it! My first paying job and the beginning of my career! I was so excited.

If you don't keep busy, you think negative thoughts. Then you become negative and make everybody around you negative. That's wrong.

You need positive things in your life. You need to be able to say, "I did that kids' workshop and, *damn*, it went well." You need things you can brag about inside yourself. Things to soup up your mind, to keep you going.

That's my drug, self-esteem.

PART IV

After living at the hotel for eighteen months, I came home one day and my mother was sitting there with a letter from welfare. They found out she saved money. The money my brothers worked hard for. The money she put aside for so many months. They said, "It's ours," and took it!

"I can't believe this," my mother said. She cried, definitely; she cried. They told her if she saved money, she could pay for the rooms at the Hotel Imperial. That would be $1,300 a month. If we didn't pay, we had thirty days to get out.

I could see my mother's eyes; she wanted to give up. She threatened us, "I'm going to put you all in a foster home." But we knew she wasn't. It was the moment.

The same day she got that welfare notice,

my mother went to look for an apartment. Morning through night, every day, she looked until she found one in Brooklyn.

"It's a regular apartment," she told us. "A tenement. We'll fix it up nice."

The apartment is on a block with abandoned buildings, a Chinese carry-out, two empty lots, and dealers. It doesn't matter. I'm busy with my life. After school, now, I volunteer at a community center. I help little kids with their homework and watch them play.

I walk in and smile at them. They say, "What are you smiling at us for? See something funny?"

"No," I say, "I want you to smile back." Too many kids have sad faces. I think when you smile, you feel happier. When you don't, you start frowning on the inside, too.

I tell them, "Sad things happen, but they don't need to bring you down. Let's think about something that was funny, like the day you fell up the stairs."

The kids used to think I'm crazy. Now they say, "Keisha, it *works!*"

On weekends I take a young journalists' class at Columbia, a university about an hour and a half from where I live. They teach us how to lay out a paper . . . interview . . . edit.

The teachers say I have a "natural instinct." And the determination.

I love writing, reporting the facts, and making up stories. But now I'm adjusting my career. My plan is to write novels. I want to be able to say, "This is my book. This is what I created — a world and its people."

Lots of people are afraid of life. I'm not. I want to challenge life. I want to express my ideas.

I'm *hot*. Yup. I'm *hot!*

3

FROM THE DIRECTOR OF AN ALTERNATIVE SCHOOL

Without goals, you wander.

— Mark Lutze, M.A.,Youth Service Bureau Learning Place, Valparaiso, Indiana

• How can you tell that you're in trouble? Here are some signs: You've been suspended or expelled from school. Drinking or using drugs is interfering with what you want to do. You've isolated yourself from adults. You listen to people you don't respect. You've been arrested.

When you're in trouble, you're constantly having to lower the goals you set for yourself. Once you might have said, "I want to be president." Then it's, "Well, maybe just senator." When you get to, "I can't finish high school," there's a problem.

• Making positive changes in a troubled lifestyle *is* hard. You probably go around with people who spend their time the same way you do. To break bad habits you might have to break from your circle of friends. And that's *real* difficult.

Also, many of you feel it's your *destiny* to not be successful. You see everything as black or white, good or bad. And you usually hear about your mess-ups, not your victories. To you, that means you're a failure.

• You communicate your problems in one way or another. If you're angry and smash mailboxes, you're likely to get into trouble.

Talk about what's bothering you, and you're almost guaranteed *not* to get in trouble. When you talk, find a listener worthy of your trust. Don't talk to the pimp on the corner about how terrible your life is.

If there's no person you feel you can trust, you might try a self-help group, maybe Alcoholics Anonymous, Narcotics Anonymous, or Families Anonymous.

Attend a meeting, and find out you're not alone in feeling weird. The kids in those groups are going through the same stuff. Together you'll discover ways to help yourself and one another.

With any of these groups, if you want it

to work, it will. If you don't want it to work, it won't. Attitude makes a difference. You can have whatever attitude you wish to have. You're in control.

• Without goals, you wander; and at first shorter-term goals are better. Goals should be realistic, and it's helpful if you can measure them. You want to know if you've attained them. If you haven't, you should figure out what obstacles are in your way.

For example, maybe your goal is to arrive on time at school every day for one week. It's easily measured. You're either there or you aren't.

Possibly the main obstacle is getting up on time. Instead of counting on a family member to wake you, take on the responsibility yourself. Don't be dependent. Buy an alarm clock, and set it. Get up when it goes off. Have a plan for what to do if you still oversleep.

• Once you're up in the morning, start with this ritual. Look in the mirror and say good things about yourself: "I am good. I can make it through this day without . . ." — whatever your problem might be. "I can do it."

Some think this positive self-talk sounds phony. Wait until you try it.

4
MOLLY, 14, A FRESHMAN

PART I

I can't tell you exactly why it started. Maybe because my father is a "gigolo," that type of man who goes with other women. I have a half-brother I never even met.

But, also, my father is an alcoholic. When he's sober, he's *great!* When he's not, I *hate* him.

There are times my mother and I go to bars to get my father. What I see, it hurts me. He's with all these women.

After that, at home, the problems really start. The alcohol changes him. He forgets he's a man with a good job that pays $18 an hour, insurance, and vacations. Alcohol starts the anger. He has to do something physical.

Sometimes he hits the wall. More often he picks up the heaviest thing around and throws it. He yells at the top of his lungs.

Next, he goes at my mother and me. He beats us to give us bruises, not to break anything. Like, we get black eyes. I'm supposed

to tell people, oh, I got in a fight with a kid.

My father has this — I don't know, feeling about women. To beat us makes him feel powerful. It keeps us in our place.

What's awful is, this is the example my little brother Ryan watches. He's a sentimental boy. I don't want him to turn into a man like my father.

My mother says it's in the family. My father's father was like this. I think, "My grandpa! Did that? He got drunk and went out with women right in front of my grandma?"

Well, my grandpa never laid a hand on my father, but my grandma did. My dad talks about taking all those beatings when he was a kid. He gets *angry!* He tells us, "I don't want you guys to grow up like I did."

In real life, what's the same is my father never hits my brother, the boy of the family. *Never.* One time I hit Ryan. Forget it. World War III. After my father whacked me and left, my mother started in. She hit *me* instead of hitting my father. This way at least it couldn't get worse.

The time she came after me with a broom, a neighbor told her, "You hit Molly again and I'm calling the law."

For some reason, I felt the fighting was my

fault. My mother said my dad's *first* other lady — whatever you want to call her — brainwashed him. She said to him, "Forget your wife. Forget your child." It got to him. He was angry my mom was pregnant with me. He beat up on her.

As I got older, I tried to get out of the way. I sat out front [of our house]. It was impossible, though, not to hear what went on between them. One time that same neighbor took me in to calm me down.

Mostly, I had to go through the embarrassment of the people on the block saying, "Hey, I heard that racket last night. . . ." Still, nobody wanted to get involved. Not even my relatives.

Every New Year's Eve, they came over. My dad would be showing off and drinking. Once, he hit my mother in front of them. "Oh, God," I thought, "can't you relatives do anything to help her?" Instead, they left.

Afterward, I said, "Oh, Mom, why don't we leave him!"

But you see, my mother is a regular housewife. She's never worked in her life. She has always depended on my father to bring home the paycheck. "I wouldn't know how to support us," she answered. "Anyway, we're Irish Catholics. Divorce is out of the question."

PART II

The good thing about me is that I'm ambitious. When I want to do something, I *do* it! I don't quit. What really helps me, too, is a teacher in sixth grade and a wonderful, caring librarian last year. In their own way, they love me.

They are both the exact portraits of people I want to be. And the great way they talk about their families! These ladies are intelligent and active. Nobody hates them. They know what they are doing. They travel. They have a profession. They are happy and single. They depend on no one but themselves.

Their words keep me going. They encourage me: "Even though you have problems, Molly, you can succeed if you try!"

I say to myself, "I will use my studies to get away from my home problems. Forget everything except school. It will make me a better person."

When the problems at home stay the same, I say, "Okay, I'll get *more* into my studies." I don't have any friends to ask for advice. And there is nothing else I can figure out to do.

What I do know, though, is right from wrong. I do know I try to keep everything straight. No bends. I live by my rules.

Rule number one: Before I take any action, I think of the consequences. Always.

I am competitive. I want to win. To do that, I think of a person I admire, who does better than I do. I say to myself, "I will get to where she is. It might take a year, but I know I can do it. If I've gotten this far, I can get even farther. Just keep my mind on it." That's rule number two: Don't give up.

Rule number three: A hobby helps. I keep myself occupied with anything — even walking. When I'm upset I walk until I calm myself. It works; I promise.

Another hobby of mine is reading. I love to read! *Go Ask Alice,* about an alcoholic, druggie girl, is the last book I read. It's excellent. I like to read books that start me thinking. I like music with messages.

PART III

The day last year I was named Teen of the Month, where my name was read over the PA and everybody congratulated me, I got home late. I was feeling so *happy*. I was feeling, *"Hey, Molly, you did it!"* It was the greatest award I could get!

I walked in the door, and my father was hitting my mother with a rolled-up newspaper.

Without thinking, I went into the fight. I tried to stop him, but it didn't do any good. I freaked out and took off, out of the house. Right away Ryan came out, screaming, *"Molly, he's hitting her harder!"*

I ran back in and tried to get between them. My dad turned on me. I thought, "It's better that he hits me. It gets him off my mother."

I started yelling, *"You're a coward! Get out of here."*

He kept hitting and yelling back, *"Mind your own business. And if you call the police, I swear I'll kill you!"* Ryan was watching, watching. I took off again — in terror.

Twenty minutes later, I looked around the corner. My father was in a police car. My mother was talking to the police, pretending like nothing that violent happened. She didn't want to get my father in trouble. That was confusing to me.

My hair was messed up. I had red bruises. I felt terrible. "Something *did* happen," I said. "Why don't we just let it out?" As they took my father away, I told the police the story.

At first, I was glad to talk. But then I thought, "Dad is going to think I called the police!" I was scared.

They took me and my brother to the police station. They wouldn't even let our mother near us. When they said they wanted to put us in a foster family, I said, "No, no. I'd rather we stay with our auntie."

They said, "Okay."

That same week, there was a court appearance. They made me and Ryan testify against our father. Oh, man, I *hated* that. He was sitting in the room. I wasn't scared of him hitting me any more. I was afraid of him hating me for the rest of his life. I didn't want to lose my dad.

Sure, he's caused me pain. But he *is* my dad. He's given me everything.

I don't like to think about it. It makes me depressed. I say to myself, maybe it's meant to be like this . . . for what finally happened . . . with the neighbor calling the police.

PART IV

It's been a year since that day in court. My father hasn't once beaten my mother or me! He's on probation. He goes to AA, Alcoholics Anonymous. He does community service, too. A program where he cleans up the litter along the highway.

He says, "The sooner I get out of these legal problems, the better."

My mom goes to this counseling stuff for battered wives. She says to me, "I guess I wanted to get my anger out, so I took it out on you."

"But it wasn't *my* fault."

"I know," she answers. "I know."

I have to go to counseling myself. A social worker comes to school to see how I'm doing. We have to do all this, or the case won't close.

School is fine, even though I don't *need* it in the same way. Now I want to have friends. I want to learn to succeed with people. And that's almost harder.

Before, I kept to myself. I didn't want to take a chance that I'd get stabbed in the back.

And the other students looked through me.

Now they see that I'm more social. I get noticed. It flips me out. I even had my first boyfriend. He was seventeen. I was wearing blue shorts and an orange half T-shirt the day we met.

My mother kept hearing, "Joey called."

"Who's that?" she said.

One day I told him to come over and meet my parents. He was nervous. They were friendly. Joey said, "They're nice."

What could I say?

In the end, Joey had too many plans for me. He wanted to go in the Marines and take me with him. Then he decided he was being selfish. "You're too young to decide those things about your future. Let's be friends."

I said, "Sure," but I couldn't see him and pretend I didn't care. I never saw him again after that conversation.

Now I'm with a new guy, Todd. I'm afraid he might cheat on me. It's not like we're married, but it would hurt.

I'm supposed to be Catholic. But the only thing I believe in is a God. When it comes to religion, I don't know if sex is wrong or right.

If I have sex, will I go to hell? I wouldn't have sex for pleasure. No way. I'd do it for love. 'Cause we really got close. It would be something that just happened.

But I'm afraid that if I ever get married, I have to tell him, "Well, I'm not a virgin." It makes me feel put down, less valued and *confused*. Religion says sex matters. What should matter is the person you are.

I know there are people around I can trust. It's just hard for me to find them.

Note: If you read this and have a story like mine, here's what I say: *Don't ignore it*. It won't stop on its own. Don't be embarrassed to try to do something to change your situation.

I wish I had said something about the violence sooner. I wish I had gotten help. I always thought it would be worse if I told some-one. That's wrong.

You're helping yourself, and your family, too.

5
FROM A GOOD NEIGHBOR

Turn the TV off, the radio off,
stop buying the three cookies
for a dollar . . . and study.

— *Cenén*

• In my neighborhood, young people say, "Go talk to Cenén. She's safe." And when kids turn to me, we fill a role for each other. As we explore their problems, they help me explore the problems I grew up with and never resolved.

When we talk, we just talk. There's no barrier to the conversation.

I tell them that the biggest obstacle I had to overcome was my mother's hate for me. She was Puerto Rican, but very white. She wanted to be white in a world where that gives you value.

My father was definitely African-looking, with dark, large lips and a flat nose. I cherished his love, but he died when I was four. My emotions became numb from the hurt.

41

• One teenager, Rosie, stops by a lot. She has a problem with her mother. Her mother doesn't speak or read English, so Rosie asked me to translate at a meeting with her teachers.

When I did, the teachers complained that Rosie did no homework. She had no idea what she was reading. Rosie's mother sent her kids to school, but she didn't say, "Do your homework."

Back then, Rosie didn't know how to talk to her mother. With her permission, I went to her mother for her. I said, "Your kids need to have quiet time at home to study."

"Yo le doy a ellos ropa limpia, comida. . . ."

"They need those things," I said, "but they also need quiet time. All your kids are failing in school."

"No puedo obligarlos a estudiar, porque el niño siempre hace ruido."

"Sit them down. Turn the TV off, the radio off, and stop buying the three cookies for a dollar. Let them be calm. Also, the older ones know more. They can help the younger ones."

• Today, a year later, the difference is amazing. But this success didn't happen overnight. At first Rosie told me, "Quiet time isn't working. Neighbors come in to gossip. We get distracted."

I said, "You wanted to grow curves, be a

cheerleader, have a boyfriend. Well, all that takes time. It's going to take time to get new and better habits."

I went back to the mother. I said, "You're bringing up low-paid office temps, soldiers for wars, and possible drug addicts! When they study, take your neighbors someplace else to gossip."

She was furious. Then she listened.

They aren't just her kids. This is the next generation, and we all live in the same world together.

• A year ago I heard Rosie tell her sisters, "As long as you get 65, it's enough." Now she says, "See this 95 I got? You can do that, too."

She shows up at school every day. That's half the battle.

Rosie has plans. She wants to be a doctor. She also knows she has to find out what it takes to prepare herself. She has to start *now* to be a doctor. She can't wait till college.

For her brother, it was important to learn to skateboard, get over, and argue his way out of situations. Now it's also important for the mother to see his papers up on the wall along with his sisters'. And pride shows in all of their faces, especially the mother's.

• In this neighborhood, we see daily horror. We find people dead in the hallways. There's even a man who lives with his whole family in a box in an empty lot across from here.

I believe we are responsible for what happens to each other. We need to help each other. Sometimes things have to be said . . . and done.

If you kids can't tell a parent or guardian what's on your mind, that they're making it impossible for you, that it's more than you can handle, that you're messing up at school because of life at home, maybe an adult you trust can help.

The pain of being alone in your fear and in your struggles for success is worse than the fear that an adult will betray you.

6

LUIS, 19, A SENIOR

PART I

My first impression of the United States was scary. I was twelve. Three guys, they're called coyotes, were helping my family escape from El Salvador to America.

It was the last part of our journey. We were in two cars following each other, driving at night through the mountains and the desert from Mexico to New Mexico.

It was a dirt road. Soon my hair and even my eyelashes were covered with dust. As we got close to the border, the coyotes turned off the headlights. "We don't want anyone to spot us," they said.

I was aware of a noise above us. An American immigration helicopter. The cars stopped. "Stay quiet," my grandfather warned me and my cousins. When we saw the helicopter fly in the other direction, we started again.

After a half hour, we came to a paved road. The two cars began to speed. I looked out the window and watched the trees go by fast. It made me sleepy.

Suddenly a siren woke me. "Speed! Speed! We must get away from them," a coyote said.

My grandfather is religious. When he prays, there's something wrong. He started to pray.

The other coyote hit the gas, but the sirens were so close to us, he pulled over. They caught the other car, too, the one with my aunt, my uncle, and another cousin.

The American immigration people took us in, fingerprinted us, and put us in jail. They kept us two weeks. Then a judge let us go on a bond or something.

My grandfather never told me exactly what happened. All I knew was we were on our way to Denver, my new home, to see my mother for the first time in seven years.

It was confusing to see my mother after that long. I didn't know her, not even how she looked. A little sister I'd never seen was there, along with a stepfather, another stranger.

After a while, everybody started saying good-bye. Me, too. I got ready to leave.

My grandfather said, "No, son, you have to stay. This is your home. Don't be afraid. She's your mother. She'll take care of you. I'll come visit."

I started to cry. My grandfather was like

my *father*, my real parent. What I remembered of my mother was that we didn't get along. Even my grandfather, her own father, said she was mean.

Here I was in a strange country surrounded by strangers. I didn't expect to come to America to be a baby-sitter for a wild, little sister. I was used to people watching over me.

"By the way," my mother said, "you sleep on the couch in the living room."

I looked out the window. I saw an old tire hanging from a tree. A guy was clapping his hands to call his dog. People were playing dice, gambling, on the sidewalk. No one was carrying baskets on their head the way they do in El Salvador. I felt far from the small village where I had lived my whole life.

PART II

For many years, there has been war in El Salvador. Still today I don't understand why it is happening. It's like there's a fire. And because there is always someone feeding it, the fire never stops burning.

I used to hear grown people talk. They said, "If only the Americans and the Russians would stop sending weapons to fight with, the war would end."

All the towns around us had been invaded

by guerrillas or the army. You never knew which. Early on, my father was killed. After that my mother came to America to look for a better life for us. She left me behind to be raised by my grandfather.

One day my grandfather and I were on the bus going to shop. The driver stopped. He saw something, he said.

There were bodies. Bodies with their heads cut off. By then it had become so common that people only said, "They dumped more people."

This didn't scare me in the daytime when I was playing. At night, though, it did. What I didn't understand then was that my grandfather was teaching me how to survive.

To calm me, he said, "Why don't you climb on the roof to see the stars?" He knew I loved to lie there and think about the mystery of the heavens. People like me up there looking back down here at us.

"And Luis, carry a handkerchief with you. If you catch a shooting star with a new cloth, you are lucky for the rest of your life."

Now that I'm older I know that in my grandfather's heart, he was scared, too. He knew what was going on with the war. Sooner or later, the men would come again with guns.

But his spirit said you should not just see the bad around you. You should also see the good things, the beautiful and simple things, like all the marañones, a yellow fruit, I could eat later.

From my grandfather, a very kind gentleman, I learned to try my best to think positive.

That first night at my mother's I thought about people who had greater problems than me. Those still in El Salvador are worried that their lives will be taken any time. They keep going. Compared to that, what I had was not such a big deal.

PART III

I have always liked school. Again, this is something I got from my grandfather. He never went to school. He doesn't know how to read or write. He doesn't know what we do in school, except that we go there to study.

His idea is that you take notes. Then you go over those notes. "On the weekends, read over all your notes," he tells me. And you know what? He's right. Doing that helps me keep up with my schoolwork.

A while ago, I had this paper to turn in. He came over to visit and saw what I was doing. He said, "Oh, that's very good. Always try to do well in school. Education is important." It makes me smile just to think of him.

But then, there's my mother. I'm not having

a good life with her. She's negative. I never get much attention from her — except to be criticized. Ever since I can remember, the first time I got a hug from her was the day I arrived. Other than that and at Christmas at midnight, when everybody hugs, nothing. It makes me feel lonely.

PART IV

Five and a half years after I come to America, the Immigration people send me a letter. For so many years I hear nothing. Now this. It is, like, a summons for me and my relatives who were caught in New Mexico.

We have to appear in court. We have to hire a lawyer.

There is confusion about immigration. The laws are changing. The lawyer we have assures us he is well informed.

"Tell the judge you will leave the U.S. on your own in a year," he says. "It's called a 'voluntary departure.' By then, everything will settle down. You qualify for amnesty and will be able to stay." We do that.

He is wrong.

A year later, the immigration people say, "You must leave the U.S. now." I ask for more time.

They say, "No. We already gave you more."

"Isn't there a family fairness law?" I say. "Any close relative of a person with a green card can't be sent back to their country? My mother has her green card. My stepfather has his."

"You are eighteen now. If we let you stay, we have to let everybody stay. We can't do that."

I work 34 hours a week at a supermarket to make $240 twice a month to save $1,000 for the lawyer to fight this for me.

I help my family out, too. My mother expects it. I don't get home until one in the morning. I have to wake up at 6:30 to get ready for school. I manage to keep my grades up. I help immigrants who can't read or write English fill out their papers. But I'm tired, and now this!

My mother adds to my worries. She makes me feel like my life is going to hell. My stepfather tells her, "Luis is not an animal. Don't treat him that way."

"Should I just kill myself?" I wonder. I know where there is poison they use to kill rats. I'll drink it.

I will end my immigration problems.

I will hurt my mother. I can watch her cry. But if I kill myself, I will cause my grandfather pain. I don't want to make him feel guilty.

51

And me? My life will go down the drain. I think of the good things, not the bad. The handkerchief and the stars.

I will show the immigration people by fighting until I win. I'll punish my mother by showing her she doesn't control me. She's not going to drive me to suicide.

I have to control myself. I'm not going to be weak.

I put the poison away and never tell anyone.

Note: Luis is still fighting to stay in the United States. Meanwhile he has been accepted at the University of Colorado–Boulder. In ten years he hopes to be an American citizen and an astronomer.

7

FROM AN OPTIMISM EXPERT

If I work hard, I will win.

— Roger Drake, Ph.D., professor of Psychology, Western State College of Colorado, Gunnison, Colorado; former Fulbright Professor, Johns Hopkins School of Medicine; expert on optimism and social psychology

• I know students with so much optimism that they don't study for a test. There are other students with extreme pessimism. They say, "There is nothing I can do." So they don't study for the test, either. Both types of students often get bad grades.

Find the middle between "I don't need to do anything, because some day I'll win the lottery," and "Everything is bad, so why even try." The kind of optimism you want says, "If I work hard, I will win."

• I'm interested in what's going on in the

brain. When you turn your eyes to the right, there is a big increase in blood flow to the left hemisphere of the brain.

It *activates* the left hemisphere. And that's where your more positive moods are, as well as your greater sense of being in control and your greater sense of optimism.

When you turn your eyes to the left, there is a big increase in blood flow to the right hemisphere of the brain. That's the more cautious side, the more conservative side.

If you want to persuade people, approach them from the left. Activate the right hemisphere. If you approach them from the right, they might think, "I don't need to change. I'm fine just the way I am."

Before you make a decision, use both your "do it" and "don't do it" parts of your brain. Look at both risk and caution. Get a good view of things before deciding whether to go ahead with things.

• Pay attention to your goals. But especially pay attention to your *subgoals*. A goal might be to earn a million dollars. A subgoal would be to earn the first $10,000. If you just wait for the million, you might never earn anything.

Know what you *really* want. People who think they want money might just want it to impress others.

• To be successful, keep patting yourself on the back. Reward yourself when you've done something important. Don't say, "Oh, well, this just happened to me by accident." Instead say, "I did that. And I'm going to do it again in other parts of my life, too."

Try to think and act and talk like a person with high achievement motivation. If you convince yourself you're going to succeed, you will.

8

PAWNEE, 18, A SENIOR

PART I

I have the same heroes that every black person has: Winnie and Nelson Mandela, Dr. Martin Luther King Jr. — people like that. But you know who my real hero is? *Myself*. And God. I guess you can't do anything without Him.

Still, you can have a thousand heroes and never do a thing. Confidence — what's inside your heart — makes the difference.

I have to be confident. I have a lot to struggle with. Especially being a teenage mom.

Before I got pregnant, I went to school, I worked, and I took care of my younger brother and sister. Both my parents work. My mom's in the office at a cab service. My father works at a place called the Superior Furniture Company. He does odd jobs. He doesn't make any more than five dollars an hour.

When he was a kid, he had to help out his family. He never finished school. I always tell him, "Why don't you go back to school, Daddy? There's a place around here you can do it." No answer.

My mom and dad were childhood sweethearts. Right after the Vietnam War, my dad came back to Los Angeles and married her. Pretty soon, I came along, and then the others.

Most kids I know, their mothers aren't married to their fathers. My mom and dad must be doing something right. They're still together.

Back then, before I was a mom, I was popular, but quiet. Life and school didn't thrill me. To tell you the truth, I wasn't thrilled, either, when I found out I was pregnant.

That was my *first* time and I got pregnant!

At first I was going to have an abortion. I was, like, "Well, I didn't ask to be pregnant. It wasn't my fault, really. I wasn't sexually active."

What made me keep it was the baby's father. I knew him since I was eleven years old, the same age my mom was when she met my dad. We didn't start going together until three years later. I thought I knew what kind of a boy he was.

I also thought he was ashamed of me. Instead, he was, "Oh, I want you to have it. I want you to have it." All that soft stuff. He stopped me from having an abortion.

★ ★ ★

Everybody always thought if I got pregnant, my momma would beat my butt. But she didn't. First, she was hurt. After that, she was supportive.

She said me being pregnant lifted her spirits. She'd been sick, and this made her feel better. From then on I always felt I was having the baby for her. She helped me a whole lot.

My dad, on the other hand, was totally upset. He said, "You're ruining your life — at fourteen." But you know, I never stopped going to school. I always had a job, too. Now he's proud.

PART II

I deal with problems as they come. I tell people: Problems are part of life. Don't sit around and worry. Deal with them. Keep trying; that's what counts.

I cried too long when I was pregnant.

When I decided to go ahead, I figured I might as well make the best of it. I didn't want to be categorized as another teen mother. Someone who didn't do anything. That depresses me. When someone says that, I say, "*Well, I'm doing it.* Teen mothers *can* make something of their lives."

I knew it was going to be hard because my

parents don't have much money. "I'd better take advantage of everything they have out here," I told myself. And I did. I still do.

I stayed in school. What's the use of dropping out? I wasn't the only one to get pregnant. But I *was* a sight to behold. I heard kids dissing me, "Miss Goodie Two Shoes. She hardly talks, so how did she make this baby?"

When I was five months pregnant, I went to another school that had special classes for pregnant teens. The girls argued and fought. They didn't care. Some of them found out their babies had the same father.

But in between the shouting, I learned a lot. There were nutrition classes, health classes, exercise classes. I started reading. I learned about the fetus and what it was like at the different times I was carrying it.

I found a place in my neighborhood called Family Helper. A lot of teen mothers go there. They tell you what's what for you and your baby.

I got on WIC, a government food program. You get extra milk and stuff before and after the baby's born. Once you find out canned milk is two dollars a can and you need thirty-one cans a month, you say *help*.

Then I thought, "Well, all the older people are having natural childbirth. I'll do the same." Me and Kareem, the father, started going to Lamaze class for natural childbirth. I dragged him there. He would be my coach when I was in labor.

By the time I went to the hospital, I knew everything. At first when the labor pains got bad, they wouldn't let Kareem in to hold my hand. I said, *"We took classes!* Here's my certificate."

Finally they said, "Okay," and he was with me for the birth.

I brought my baby, Jasmine, home to our little three-bedroom house. My parents have one room. Me and Jasmine share a room. My sister has another, and my brother sleeps on a rollaway bed.

Kareem would stay over sometimes that first year. He wasn't doing anything, anyway. He would watch her while I would sleep. Right then on weekends I had a job at Taco Bell, too. Once I had two jobs at a time. I'm not one to ask my parents for money.

But I was tired. I'd be so tired, I'd be sleeping in school. I told my girlfriends, *"Don't have kids!"* But within months after I had my baby, they *all* got pregnant — every last one of them.

I told my sister, "Being a teen parent *isn't* easy. I don't want to see you end up like me."

But she got jealous of Jasmine. Before, I spent a lot of time with my sister. Took her places. Bought her clothes. Now I was trying to teach her responsibility. I wanted her to watch Jasmine when I went out. I'd pay her.

Soon, though, she was out of control.

I live in the inner city. It's hard to hide Jasmine from the drugs, cursing, and people walking around half-naked. She sees so much. It depresses me to bring her outside.

I think if she doesn't see it at home, maybe she'll think outside is different. I encourage her, "Don't drink or smoke. It's not good for you."

My father, he's been drinking most of his life. The War — that's why he drinks. He never talks about it. Not at all.

I say to him. "Dad, don't come home like that if you're going to drink."

A couple times my baby says, "Granddaddy, you shouldn't be drinking." After that, my dad never takes a drink around her. Now the only people she sees drinking at home are on Kareem's side of the family.

His mother and brothers all drink and smoke. And they do it in front of her. I don't like that, but I can't stop them. Still I tell her over and over, "You don't see Mommy doing it." I don't want to pressure her. I'm just giving her things to think about and look forward to.

PART III

My baby, she has to be my focus. She's got to have the best. I really give her love, love, love and reach for the stars.

I buy her educational toys and ninety-nine-cent books. I play with her. I read to her. Now she goes to her toy chest and gets a book. She don't know what she's reading, but she goes through it. It's a start.

I talk to people with kids. They say, "You're buying your baby stuff every week. Where'd you get the money for it?"

Well, I'm a sales fanatic when it comes to clothes, too. I found a baby store that sells name-brand used clothes. They look as good as new.

I see my baby's name — JASMINE SHER-INE LANGSTON — up in lights. I pretend; it doesn't hurt. I psych myself up to believe lots of things. My fantasy world helps keep me going.

That's what I think about when I get up at six in the morning. I get out our clothes. Then I wake Jasmine and get her ready. I take her to day care. Then I go to school.

Family Helper found me an organization

that wants teen mothers to stay in school. As long as I maintain a C average, they pay for my day care. Child care is good with her. They feed her, get her plump, but I wish they had more time to sit down and read to the babies. I want Jasmine to *learn.*

And I want to learn. I go to a school where there are lots of different nationalities. I like that. But it's hard to do everything. My grades are slipping. First I was an A and a B student. Now I'm more a C student. But I haven't failed anything!

When Jasmine turned one, Kareem left. I couldn't get over it. I never did anything wrong to him. I'm so nice. I'd make a good wife. That's the way I treated him, like my husband. Why can't he love me and love the baby?

Why can't we . . . not start a family, but have the family that we have now?

I get depressed. I sleep late and get up too late and, maybe, miss the two required courses I need. "If Kareem could help me, maybe I could leave one of my jobs," I think.

He was there the first year. What happened? I feel tired all the time. I psych myself up to believe that one day he'll come back . . . and then, and then . . . I'll slap him in the face!!

My favorite teacher says, "Pawnee, I'm worried about you. Are you okay?" Inside I'm a total wreck.

Gradually, I start saying to myself "Everything happens for the best. It's going to take awhile, but I'm going to get over it. I'm not going to let anything bring me down. I'm not going to worry about it. I got this far by myself; I'll just keep going."

It never crossed my mind that Kareem would just up and disappear. I see my old girlfriends. One of them got married. One of them made the father keep the baby; she's on the streets. The third one's boyfriend is a caring father. All of them have good daddies, except me! And I was the first one pregnant.

PART IV

I feel stronger now. Jasmine is three. It used to *really* bother me what people thought of me. I cried. But now, I don't care. I learned, honey, if you care about what people think, you'll be under your grave.

They see me in the health clinic, and they assume I'm pregnant again.

"I'm too smart for that," I tell them. "I'm *not* going to make the same mistake twice!"

Now girls, here's a piece of advice: do *not* depend on a man. You never know how long he's going to be there. That's why I started gathering all this information — myself. In my heart I must have known Kareem might not be here forever.

Here's some more. Try to stand on your own two feet. Keep an open mind. Don't let the negative bother you. And if you have a real good older person, or even somebody young that's real positive, talk to them. That's helped me, too.

I notice that most teenagers don't like to listen to older people. I do. I like to talk to them. They fascinate me. They be looking at me, like, "I've been here a lot *longer* than you. And I know more."

Those older people I look up to say, "Pawnee, you should go to college."

I think, I don't want to hurt their feelings, but I'm not ready for it. Sure, success in school is fine. But for me, it's important to succeed as a person. I want to be the best, most loving, helpful, supportive mom I can be.

I want to succeed for my baby, my Jasmine. I just *have* to do it for her. I want her to be able to say when she goes to school, "I don't have a daddy. But my mom, she was a teen mom, and I'm so *proud* of her."

Everybody says God puts people on the

world for something. Maybe that's why I'm here. Maybe I'm supposed to be Super Mom! Then after that, I'll open my own day-care center.

9
FROM A PROBATION OFFICER

Read.

— Michael Leonard, Community Resource and Training Specialist, Kings (County) Juvenile Offender Program, Brooklyn, New York

• I lived in the Red Hook projects in Brooklyn until I was twenty-two. Sometimes it seemed like everybody around me was getting high or committing crimes. I watched friends die.

I was fortunate, though. My mother and my father kept us so busy we didn't have time to get into trouble. Then, at seventeen, I decided I wanted to help my neighbors.

While some people in my community were guilty of crimes, I also saw others who were railroaded. I felt that more blacks should be involved in making the criminal justice system better. Today I'm trying to do that.

Now when I work with the kids in the juvenile offender program, kids who've committed violent crimes like rape, arson, burglary, manslaughter, I say, "There but for the grace of God go I." I do what I can to help them.

• One of the exercises in our program is to make a Life Chart. It might help you succeed, too. The first thing you do is draw stick figures of your family on a blank sheet of paper. Use the male (♂) and female (♀) symbols and show where you fit — oldest, middle, whatever.

Now along the side put in some age ranges, say, zero to three, four to six, seven to nine. Draw symbols to highlight the events that took place in your life. You'll forget some at first. When you remember, add them next to the right age ranges.

My Life Chart has a picture of a bat. That's the name of the first book I ever read with no one telling me I had to. From the age of nine to twenty-three, I was a Muslim. I included a picture for that. In high school, I was stopped by a cop in the park. That picture's there, too.

Then you use these charts and the symbols to talk about your lives. Lots of you have never dealt with these events. And they're stopping you. They're barriers between you and success. If you talk about them, you get out your anger *and* discover how important your life is.

Add your *future* goals on the bottom line. They're important, too. You take what I call a futuristic walk. Think about not only graduation, but *after* graduation. Think about after that first job, even *after* that second job. . . .

There's a different conversation for those of you without a future and those of you with one. The kids without a future talk about what they *used* to do. The kids with a future talk about what they *want* to do. They are the ones who will succeed. They believe there is hope instead of dope.

The person you talk to about this Life Chart should be someone who cares. Look for a peer counselor, an adult counselor, or just somebody who will direct you in a positive way.

• Create a list of goals. Read it. Memorize it. Repeat it every day. This is an example of what one of the groups here came up with.

"I realize that the power to change my life lies within me. It is my goal to produce this change. I will do the following:

"I will stay out of trouble.

"I will accept positive advice.

"I will think and act in positive ways.

"I will successfully structure my talents and hobbies.

"I will successfully complete high school and attend college.

"I will obtain a high-paying job other than selling drugs.

"I will live a long, prosperous life."

You need to confess what you want to be. Learn to say, "I am the smartest thing that ever walked the face of this earth. I am creative, imaginative, important."

Many of you have always been told you're stupid. You'll never learn. If you hear that long enough, you believe it.

Start looking at that negative stuff and ask yourself, "Why do I feel like s__t? I'm a good person."

Every time you begin to feel bad about yourself, change the message in your head. Say, "I know I'm okay."

Confront the person telling you, "You aren't important." You *are* special.

• One last word — *read*. More than half the kids in our program read below a fifth-grade level. And I'm talking about kids fifteen, sixteen years old. It's horrible. Choose to learn how to improve your reading.

10
SUZANNE, 14,
A FRESHMAN

PART I

My boyfriend, Chas, asks me why I'm pulling away from him. "I'm not," I say. "I'm just expecting something."

"What do you mean?" he says.

"Every other relationship I've been in, it hasn't been ten minutes, and I've gotten hurt. Two months have gone by with you and me. What's the story? I'm so used to getting hit or screamed at. . . ."

He looks at me and says, "I'd never do that."

"I've heard that before."

"Well, has it happened yet?"

"No. But I'm still waiting." And then I start to cry.

I cry a lot.

He says, "What's wrong?"

"If you only knew."

I could be thinking about my dad. My stepmom. Being on self-destruct. The detox program I just finished. It seems never-ending.

Right then I was thinking about my half-sister Francine. I just saw her for the first time since she was itty-bitty. Nearly ten years ago. She looked like my mom. Really pretty. A redhead with freckles and green eyes. It scared me to death.

Almost the first question Francine asked was, "Why did your dad kill my mom — our mom?"

I said, "What are you talking about? He's not the one who did it."

She went, "How do you know?"

"I was there . . . and so were you. But I saw it. You were just a month old then. I'm the only one to witness the whole thing."

"Gramma always tells me that your father was in the house and shot my mom."

"It wasn't like that," I said, since I've *always* had memories of that day. They never go away.

"Okay, so what happened?" she asked. I told her.

I was four. To me the house we lived in then was real big. It was a split-level. In the backyard were swings and a sandbox. I lived there with my mom and my dad until I was two. When they divorced, my so-called step-

72

father moved in.

My mom was an alcoholic and addicted to Valium. She had three or four doctors all prescribing it for her. She never thought she had a drug problem.

When she got pregnant, she had trouble. . . . I stayed with my grandparents until my little sister was born. Then I was sent back home.

I remember little things: my mom doing the dishes. "Go upstairs and bring down the glasses," she'd tell me. They'd be all over the place. There were empty bottles, too, liquor bottles.

The weirdest thing was that my mom had this gun sitting on her bedside table. It was a handgun, a .44, I guess.

You could say I had clues of what she was going to do. That day we were sitting together on the couch, watching "Sesame Street." I had this toy clock. She was teaching me how to tell time.

After a while she went to the kitchen for something to drink. She came back out and said, "Well, I'm tired. I want to go upstairs to nap. Don't bother me."

And then she paused. She turned around and took my hand. She said, "If anything happens to me, I want you to pick up the phone and press the zero. Wait for someone to answer and tell them what happened."

It seemed real quiet upstairs. I was nosey. My stepfather was at work. The baby was asleep. I was, like, what *is* Mom doing?

I set down my toy clock and tiptoed up the stairs. At the last step, I stopped, looked straight ahead and there was Francine in her crib. I looked into my mom's room.

She was sitting there with the gun pointed at her heart.

She saw me and said, "I want you to leave! *Now!*"

"What are you doing?"

"Leave now!" she went.

As I turned around, she pulled the trigger and fell on the floor.

Francine started to cry.

I remembered what my mom had told me about the phone. I ran downstairs, pressed zero, and kept screaming, "I was upstairs with my mom and she shot herself! *She shot herself!*" The lady, the operator, didn't believe me at first.

She asked my address. I *knew* my address. My mother taught me that, too. But I froze. I couldn't remember.

I tried to open the front door to look at the numbers in front of the house. The deadbolt lock was on. Finally, the operator traced the call and sent an ambulance. These guys came breaking through the windows and the back door. "We'll take it from here," they said.

The next thing I knew there was a stretcher with a white sheet over my mom. And a bloodstain, I remember the bloodstain. They carried her out. Then my grandmother showed up and took me and Francine to her house.

It's a total blur from then to the funeral, when I threw up all over the place. They said, "We have to pay respects to your mom."

There are so many confusing things from when I was a kid. I remember parts. Like the custody battle for me between my dad and my gramma. I had to go to the courthouse in Greensboro, the town where we lived.

This guy, my gramma's lawyer, asked me, "Who do you want to live with?" I was so scared I ran right by him to my grandmother. I held onto her and cried.

The next thing I remember I was back at their house. Within days, though, my father took me. Legally. The courts said he could.

My dad came to pick me up. We walked out of my grandparents' house, and he threw my stuff in the back seat of his Volvo. "Get in," he told me.

My grandfather ran up and started to choke

him. They really got into it. Pretty soon, my dad broke loose. We took off to his house in Norfolk, Virginia.

To this day, I don't know why he wanted me to live with him. He has an important job at a bank, but he's a drinker, just like my mom. He's also the kind to tell me I'm capable of doing things, and the next day, he says, "You're not capable at all."

I don't believe he's ever wanted me to succeed. When I go to succeed, I often end up stopping. I'm scared that I won't be able to do what I'm supposed to do.

"Oh, you're just like your mom. She was a total screw-up." He tells me that, too. Well, if I'm like her, I think, why should I try? I might end up like her.

Then I go, "My mom wasn't a stupid person. She was a college graduate." She met my dad when they were both working their way through school. He was the counter man in a diner, and she was waiting tables.

"I will *not* commit suicide," I tell myself.

You know, she hurt me. She left me behind.

My dad and this lady, my new stepmom, told me to forget about my mother, forget about my grandparents. I was there to stay. I looked at them, like, excuse me?

My stepmom was young and, at the time,

didn't have any kids. She didn't want me there. For the coming years — when I was seven and eight and nine — she made that clear.

She told me I was terrible. I was a brat. I should go to my room and stop that crying. I was invading her space. I was hurting her relationship with my dad.

"I don't deserve to be treated this way," I told her.

No one else seemed to care what went on inside that house. People would meet my dad and stepmom and think they were the sweetest parents on the face of the earth.

He's a banker! No one ever expected him to be as mean as he is. No one ever expected him to do anything wrong. Whenever I tried to tell anybody how I felt, they looked at me and said, "Oh, not your dad and stepmom."

For a while, about a year or two ago, they talked a lot about a divorce. I was like — whatever. That was my attitude toward life. I felt trapped.

When they were really fighting, he sexually abused *me* and everything. When she threatened to move out, he stopped. That confused me, too.

I hated my stepmother with a passion. But then my dad beat her up real bad. I felt sorry for her. I didn't want to see her in pain. On the other hand, I wanted her out of my life.

I knew all the pain she had caused me. Off and on, though, she wanted me to accept her as my mother. But she wasn't. And I wouldn't. I knew who my mom was. She wasn't the one. I didn't know how to feel!

PART II

By the time I was in seventh or eighth grade, I lost interest in school. I didn't want to learn anything. I didn't care about anything. I had lots of friends, though. I was the class clown.

The biggest geeks, the kids walking the halls with their heads down — I made their day, too. They made me think of myself. How bad I felt inside.

But with my shield on, everybody thought everything in my life was fine. See, on the surface, I had what I wanted. All the attention in the world.

Since my parents kept cutting me down and my friends never did, at least not to my face, I decided friends were more important. I didn't know you can't just give yourself to a group of people, like I did.

I did Valium like my mom had. I drank anything and everything, like both my parents. All the kids at school I hung out with

78

did drugs and drank.

My dad told me, "Suzanne, you're worthless." I took his words out on myself. I rubbed my arm back and forth until it bled. I have scars, and it didn't even hurt.

When it came to dealing with my family, I didn't know how. Or I remembered how, but was scared. I hadn't done it in so long. Maybe I'd just give up and not bother. That's how I was thinking.

The guy I was going out with back then — Michael — was the one who made the difference. I was a mature thirteen, but I *was* thirteen, as my stepmom would point out. And he was eighteen. He was also bigger and stronger and could bully people around. He was over six feet tall and weighed two hundred and twenty pounds. I felt safe with him. Except when he got angry.

Michael threw me around a few times. But I told myself, "He's an abused kid, too. He doesn't understand if you get mad at someone you're not supposed to belt them so hard they fall down the stairs. He wasn't taught differently."

I excused his behavior, thinking, "Things will get better."

I thought about him more than I thought about anybody, myself included. Once I even thought about having his kid. I told my-self no. I was too scared about how it would turn out. I didn't want to put a kid in the position I was and keep that abusive cycle going.

I've been through it and I know what it feels like. In a lot of ways, abuse is still there . . . knocking at my door. I realized if I had a kid, it could be the key to that door.

Anyway, I'd seen Michael for five days straight. I wanted to see him again. My stepmom said, "You're not going out with him tonight."

"Oh, but I am," I said.

"Listen to me, young lady. You're staying in, or you're grounded till the end of the month."

"I'm going whether you like it or not."

"He's a bad influence on you. He does drugs."

"So what else is new?" I said.

Pretty soon we were in this catfight. She grabbed my head. I threw her over the couch. Then suddenly, my stepmom left.

She didn't come home that night. I thought my dad was going to beat me up. I went to school the next day. When I came home, *no-body* was there. I was terrified.

I talked to Michael. "Leave," he told me. I listened to anything he said. I left.

PART III

At 3:18 P.M. the next day, I turned myself into the hospital. It has a program for problem children, so to speak. If your parents don't know what to do with you, they send you there. I knew I was in trouble, even if they didn't.

At first, I was admitted as a runaway. Then I was a drug addict/alcoholic in the detox program. I was there for three months — the amount of time covered by my dad's insurance.

I was also there because I *had* to be. You could call it a turning point. A click in my head. I don't know exactly what changed. Everything had built up. It was constant — my dad, my stepmom, the drugs. I had to face life — cold.

I went on dry drunks, at first. Without taking a drink, I acted the same and had the same attitude. I woke up in cold sweats. I had flashbacks. They put me on this medication that I didn't think had any effect. Then I'd be walking down the hallway and think I was somewhere else. Weird.

Right in the beginning, I missed Michael. He wanted to break me out, but I told him no. Then he went on and on about how he was going to wild parties. Jerk.

I had my first therapy and blew the lady off — stay away from me. I don't want to talk to you. But then I started to realize I was there to take care of myself, not think about Michael.

In the hospital they drain your brain to the point where you have to think. They bring things to your attention. They help you think about what has gone on around you.

Like, I began to realize that for a long time I have been under the influence of something — some person, some drug, or both.

I also started to see that if I know deep down that I can succeed and don't try, then I hurt myself like other people hurt me. I learned — don't do to myself what others are doing to me.

Instead of focusing on everything that everyone in my family is doing, I focus on myself. I decided, my dad is wrong. If I set my mind to it, I *am* capable of doing just about anything that I want to.

Just because he and my stepmom are always telling me I'm terrible, I don't have to believe them. I know lots of things about life. And it isn't just stuff that I read out of books. It's things that have happened to me.

I look inside myself, and decide this is who

I am. This is who I want to be. Nobody can change that but me. If I think something is right and it's positive, I should act on it. I should say to myself, this is what I want to happen. I shouldn't allow people to push me around.

Then there's my mom's suicide. I'm trying to understand it wasn't my fault. I felt guilty for the longest time. It was my job, I thought, to take care of her. No one else was there.

I say to myself, "It's not like I was the one who said, 'I want to die.' " I didn't cause it. Even though it hurts, I have to move on. I can't drive myself so down in a hole that I can't get out. And in my struggle to get out, I can't let all the dirt fall back in.

I *have* to do something for myself. I have to prove to myself that just because something like that happened, I *can* move on.

I know; it's hard.

PART IV

I'm out of the hospital now, back in school. Maybe for the first time I care about school. I like my classes. What's hard now is I *don't* want to give up. Every time I think about giving up, I think *no way*.

But I feel I've changed, and my parents haven't. I'm still having trouble getting along with them. We have so many differences in the way we think.

Since I'm home, I see a therapist once a week. He wants my dad and my stepmom to come, too. Usually they don't show up. "Well, your dad has to work." "Your stepmom needs her sleep." "The dog got sick."

Last weekend my stepmom wasn't home. That gave my dad the leeway to do what he wanted. He got drunk. I'm just out of detox, and he's getting drunk as a skunk.

You know when you're little, maybe you pull up some grass in your yard. What's showing, the top of it, looks great. But the underside, what you usually don't see, that's all mud and worms. That's how I sometimes see myself . . . and other people. Like my new boyfriend, Chas.

He lost both his parents. His dad got drunk one night. Shot his mom and then turned around and shot himself. Now he lives with his uncle, a mean man.

Chas will go a week of great grades, great participation in class. Then there are other weeks where he allows his uncle to get him down so low that he doesn't know if he should keep trying or if he should just give up and die.

His uncle came to school the other day. He

was making a complete ass out of himself. When he was finally done, Chas looked at him and said, "Can we go home now?"

It wasn't, *"You S.O.B.!"* He controlled himself.

I told him, "Chas, you handled that well." I wanted to let him know that when he did that, somebody *did* see it. I'm learning from Chas. I'm learning that getting my life together comes in very small steps.

I see it as success if I keep my grades up. It's a success if I *don't* harm myself.

Some days I'm still scared of success. I used to run from everything. Now physically I may not be running, but mentally maybe I am.

I know if I don't want to deal with all this, no one can pin me down and force me. Some days I'm not sure what's keeping me here. I want to give up on school, on success.

I know if I go down the street, there's a phone booth. I can get money and go buy more Valium, more blacks, more whatever. I can put on that shield again. Not let anyone in. How thick does it have to be to keep me from getting hurt?

I'm not used to putting myself first. I just have to understand that's what I have to do. I have to learn that people you love sometimes disappoint you.

There's a lot of pressure on me from my

teachers and my therapist. These are people who know I can succeed. I feel if I let them down, it's going to hurt me bad.

I've been let down so many times before, I'm scared if I let them down, I don't know how they'll look at me. I know they're not going to hate me. I know they're not going to beat me. But I feel a responsibility to succeed.

And then there's Chas. I finally feel I found someone I can trust. I'm beginning to let myself open up to that. Still, it's hard for me to accept that people care.

This afternoon I'm feeling down. Chas gives me a hug and says, "I want you to repeat after me."

I look at him, like, great, here we go.

"I want you to say, 'There is a person around me who cares.' "

I go to say it, and my throat chokes up. I can't say it. In my mind, I accept it. In my heart, it takes time.

11
FROM A STRESS EXPERT

You aren't your experiences. You are what you make of them.

— Deborah Belle, Ed.D., assistant professor of psychology, Boston University; the William T. Grant Foundation Faculty Scholar in the Mental Health of Children; expert on stress and families, Boston, Massachusetts

• I'm a professor of psychology and a researcher. There is research that shows that for kids having trouble in school, one of the best things they can do is tutor younger kids. You learn so much and feel so good from this experience. Even those with behavior problems with peers benefit from playing with younger kids.

One of the stupid things about our society is that we're so age graded, you almost never get a chance to do that. For those of you with troubles, try to find a way to be given a chance to help others.

You work out your own life when you help someone else.

• Here are a few more things that research seems to show: To succeed, it's helpful to have a mentor. If you can find any positive person — a teacher, a swimming instructor, an uncle, a godmother. These figures are powerful.

Kids have more difficulty when they lack the same sex parent in the home. If that's the case with you, find a support figure who's your same sex.

Another thing that seems to help is if you think about your life, make decisions, and then come up with a plan. Don't rush pell-mell without thinking.

• All the estimates of violence, death, divorce, and so on, are appalling. And we have an unfortunate way of dealing with these issues. We ask, "How severely damaged were you by this?"

The fact is they become part of your life and change your life. But they can sometimes change you in a positive way. Look at the lives of great people. You often find that they coped with terrible tragedies.

You can take those experiences, turn them around, learn from them, and grow more connected. Speak of yourself not as a victim, but as a survivor.

You aren't your experiences. You are what you make of them.

CHAPTER 12

DANIEL, 16, A JUNIOR

HIS
STORY
IN
WORDS
AND
PICTURES

SOMETHING INSIDE ME SNAPPED. I WENT INTO THE CLOSET AND CAME OUT WITH MY STEPFATHER'S GUN.

MY STEPFATHER WAS ABOUT TO HIT MY MOM AGAIN. I POINTED THE GUN AT HIS HEAD. I WAS 14.

AS I STOOD THERE, MY MIND FLASHED BACK TO GRAMMAR SCHOOL WHERE I'D BEEN HAPPY.

I LIKED SHOW AND TELL. THE TEACHERS WERE NICE. THEY TAUGHT US COMMON SENSE AND VALUES.

MY FAVORITE TEACHER SAID, "IF YOU LET PEOPLE RUN YOU WHEN YOU KNOW BETTER, YOU'RE TRAPPED."

I FELT I HAD A GIFT. THERE WAS THIS VOICE INSIDE MY HEAD. IT TOLD ME RIGHT FROM WRONG.

91

THEN, TWO YEARS AGO, MY MOM CAME BACK FROM A TRIP AND SAID, "I MET THIS NICE MAN."

THE NEXT THING I KNEW, THEY WERE MARRIED.

AND WITHIN DAYS HE WAS HITTING, HER, I WAS DYING. HE HIT HER! I DIDN'T UNDERSTAND. SHE LOVED HIM.

SHE THOUGHT HE LOVED HER. WHY WAS HE DOING THIS? SHE ONLY WANTED TO BE WITH HIM.

HE TAUGHT ME TO HATE. HE SAID THE WORLD WOULD HURT ME IF I DIDN'T HURT IT FIRST.

HE WAS A GUN AND MARTIAL ARTS FANATIC. HE TOOK OUT HIS ANGER AND FRUSTRATION ON LIFE.

92

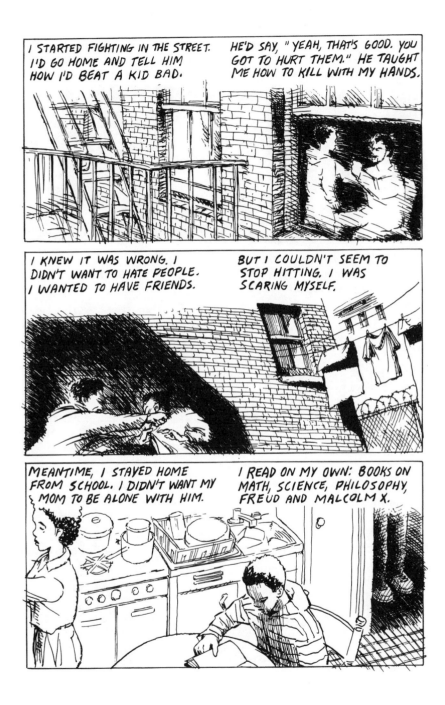

I STARTED FIGHTING IN THE STREET. I'D GO HOME AND TELL HIM HOW I'D BEAT A KID BAD.

HE'D SAY, "YEAH, THAT'S GOOD. YOU GOT TO HURT THEM." HE TAUGHT ME HOW TO KILL WITH MY HANDS.

I KNEW IT WAS WRONG. I DIDN'T WANT TO HATE PEOPLE. I WANTED TO HAVE FRIENDS.

BUT I COULDN'T SEEM TO STOP HITTING. I WAS SCARING MYSELF.

MEANTIME, I STAYED HOME FROM SCHOOL. I DIDN'T WANT MY MOM TO BE ALONE WITH HIM.

I READ ON MY OWN: BOOKS ON MATH, SCIENCE, PHILOSOPHY, FREUD AND MALCOLM X.

I ASKED MY SCHOOL FOR TUTORING HELP. I'D GO TO THE TUTORS' HOUSES AT NIGHT WHEN MY...

... STEPFATHER WASN'T HOME. SOMETIMES HE PUNISHED ME WHEN I CAME HOME LATE.

WHEN HE BROKE MY MOM'S JAW I WAS REALLY FREAKING. THERE WAS BLOOD ALL OVER.

SHE WASN'T THE SAME AFTER THAT.

I COULDN'T HELP HER, I COULDN'T EVEN HELP MYSELF. I WANTED TO GIVE UP.

THE VOICE IN MY HEAD SAID, "THAT'S NOT WHO YOU ARE." BUT I THOUGHT, "WHO CARES!"

I HELD THE GUN STEADY AND SAID TO MY STEPFATHER, "STOP OR I'LL KILL YOU."

AS I SPOKE THOSE WORDS, I THOUGHT, "I AM MESSING UP, FOLLOWING IN HIS FOOTSTEPS."

"I AM ABOUT TO KILL SOMEONE. AM I REALLY READY TO GIVE UP ON MY OWN FUTURE?

"AREN'T I BETTER THAN THIS? CAN'T I STILL PICK MYSELF UP AND BE SOMEBODY?"

MY STEPFATHER SMILED AT ME AND SAID, "I'M JUST TALKING TO HER."

I PUT THE GUN DOWN. I PICKED UP THE PHONE AND CALLED MY GRANDPARENTS IN CLEVELAND.

13
FROM A HIGH SCHOOL TEACHER

Don't tell me you can't do it. . . . There's always a way.

— Jan Crain, director, drama department; teacher, English literature and magnet teacher training academy; adviser, drill team, Crenshaw High School, Los Angeles, California

• In my years of teaching, whether the teenager wants to be an actor, a scientist, or just get out of the house to survive, what often drives them is that someone told them, "You won't succeed."

Do people tease *you,* put you down, and tell you that you're fat, ugly, or can't be part of their clique? Let their words spur you on to prove them wrong. Make "I can" be your motto.

To succeed, remember that there's always a way. Sometimes you just forget how talented you are.

• Every year in my classes, we take long sheets of paper and draw around each student. We cut out those life-size models and put them around the room. Next I write in large letters "I AM." "What are your talents?" I ask. "Are you — a good cook? A good friend? Smart? Honest? Loyal?"

They put on their own model all the words that describe whatever they think they are. So from then on, the first thing they see when they walk in the door is their own paper cut-out reminding them they *are* someone.

You can make one, too. Tape it to a place where you can see it and remember your value.

• Everybody can't be a good student, but maybe you run track, do hair, or make your own clothes. Or maybe you're an honor student *and* have a smile that stops a train, but there's no one who cares, especially no one at home.

I try to stay in tune with the things that my students do well in, other than my class. I compliment them, tell them to "go with it." At the same time, they know I'm a single mother with three kids. I ask them for advice and feedback. This way they sometimes talk about their problems.

You could have this give-and-take with your friends, too. We *all* need to think that we're valued. Being complimented for our talents keeps us going.

It also helps build self-esteem. With self-esteem, you have the first lifeline to hold on to. No matter what wave hits you, you have something to ride it with. Remember, though, while self-esteem is great, that alone doesn't mean you can solve problems. Self-esteem can't give you good judgment.

• Lots of kids are doing more compensating than living. High school is no longer three years of dances, parties, and stuff. You work to pay rent and utilities to live at home. Then you come home not knowing what you might have to deal with. There's no structure. No routine.

You're taught no values, no manners.

You take things without asking, without saying "please" or "thank you." You walk down the hallway, hit a girl, and never think to apologize. You go someplace in public and are loud and rude. And you don't even know that to succeed in this world, to succeed as a person, you can't act that way.

To change that, watch someone — maybe a grandmother, a neighbor, a teacher — who has good manners. Use that person as a model for the polite way to do things.

14
RULA, 16, A JUNIOR

PART I

My parents come from the Middle East, the country of Jordan. They are Muslim. I am, too. Even when I was younger, and kids made fun of me for my religion, I was proud of who I was.

The Muslim religion is strict and has lots of rules. Take food. You can't eat ham, bacon, or pork. During the holy month, Ramadan, you can eat only after sunset.

Every day you pray five different times, and the men pray separately from the women. Good Muslim women have no part of their body showing, except a little bit of the face.

My parents have lived in America for twenty years. Still, they try to be a traditional Muslim family. They don't want us kids to be Americanized. My father says, "We stay within our own community."

But I was born and raised here, in Detroit, Michigan. My views on life, and especially on women, are different from theirs.

I like to know *everything* about *everybody*. I know lots of teenagers hate school. I like it. To me, it's always been fun. And I know education is the road to a good future.

My teacher in third grade had a spark. She was positive and pushy in a nice way. That made me feel positive, too. She gave me dignity.

In school I learned it's best to stay on top of things. I do all my work when I get the assignments. If I put it off, I feel pressurized.

If I want to succeed, I can't wait around for it to happen. I have to get up and do something. Then I will achieve my goals and nobody can conquer me.

My favorite class is U.S. history.

I never missed a day of school until last year, when I was a sophomore. That was because my parents forced me to marry.

PART II

My mother and father never sat me down and said, "Rula, it's Muslim tradition for us to pick your husband." I just kind of knew. But when they said, "We have arranged a marriage for you," I was *shocked*.

How could they make me marry a Jordanian man twice my age? This was America!

I told my father, "I respect you and the

Muslim culture. But this isn't right for me."

I had never talked back to him before. I was afraid of him. He and Allah — God — were the only ones I feared.

"The man's well off," my father said. "He's the *perfect* person."

He called me rebellious, an unruly child.

The more I talked, the stronger I felt. I bugged him and bugged him. "Marriage is a commitment for life. I'm not ready. I want to go to school. I have plans. I have dreams for the future — my future."

"Females don't get anything from school. You don't need an American education."

"Oh, yes, I do!" I answered, hoping he would break and let me have my way.

PART III

I got married in a fancy white dress in front of 250 people from the Muslim community. It was a *nightmare.*

And from that first night, it was fight after fight with the man I married. He told me the role of the Muslim wife. "You have children. You nurture them. You nurture me, your husband. You cook, clean, and take care of the house."

"I know, I know," I said. "But there's more to me than just the home. I want to be a college history teacher, too."

"The Muslim husband wears the pants in the family. He goes out, works, and brings money home to the wife. A Muslim wife doesn't work outside the home unless there is a time of need. Then she helps. You, my wife, will do what I say."

In my soul, I knew that that was not the life for me. Later, yes, at twenty-five, twenty-six, I hope to marry. But then it will be to someone of *my* choice!

I missed being in school. I missed my friends. And I really missed David, the guy I was going with behind my parents' backs. He was so cute. Gorgeous brown eyes and olive-brown skin, my color. He was six feet three and had his life ahead of him.

I was in prison. What could I do?

I knew! I studied in school about the government and American history. I *knew* I had certain rights under the United States Constitution.

Secretly, I called my favorite teacher and asked, "What exactly can I do? I was forced to marry a man I don't even know."

"Go to a lawyer," he said, and gave me a name to call.

That's what I did. The lawyer he recommended guided me through every step. Two months after the wedding ceremony, I sued to have the marriage annulled.

It was scary. My family and I had to go into court. My father was outraged. Who could have dreamed I'd do something like this?

The judge said to him, "Your daughter needs to respect your customs. But you need to learn more about her. You need to respect her goals and plans for the future."

My father said, "I'm only trying to do what I think is best for her. Later on in life, she'll learn who made the mistake."

The judge said my marriage did not exist. It was annulled. I went back home to live with my family.

PART IV

"You shamed us," my parents keep saying. "You shamed us in front of our Muslim community. We can no longer walk outside with pride."

This isolates me from my brothers and sisters, too. I am on my own. I am an outsider in my own family. Who knows? This may be better. All of us are on our own out in the world.

Today, I am clear inside. Once more I'm building for my future. I have learned from this experience: There is always a solution to a problem. I will get through it. I won't let it burden me.

If I feel I'm losing faith, Allah is there. And I know if I have the determination to succeed, I *will*. If I don't believe in myself, no one else will. But when others see that I'm determined, they will help me.

I am the only one of me. And I'm special.

15
FROM A PSYCHIATRIST

You must have a sense of your own future.

— *Pearl Gong, M.D., general and child psychiatrist, Long Island Jewish Medical Center–Hillside Hospital; Project Outreach, a substance abuse program, West Hempstead, New York*

• I was born and raised in New York City. My parents were from China. Because they never completely learned English or their way around the city, my siblings and I became their baby-sitters.

When I was in junior high, a counselor found out that a couple of private schools gave scholarships to ghetto kids. It was an amazing chance for me.

At first I thought being an Asian-American was an obstacle for me in a private school. I discovered the bigger obstacle was the class difference. My family was poor and not sophisticated. Here were wealthy, educated, and powerful people. Their life-style and way of dealing with things were totally different.

Later, I came to understand the sadness, too. Many kids had all the money in the world, but their parents were divorced or off somewhere. The kids didn't know where. They felt abandoned.

• If you want to succeed and your parents are in your way, possibly you can get support from an aunt or a cousin, someone you can relate to and confide in.

I had a supportive grandmother, and that made a difference. She lived a couple blocks away. My mother worked with her in their laundry. We were down there and saw her a lot.

I also had a stand-in family. My best girlfriend was Puerto Rican. I stayed at her house all the time. I felt her family was more nurturing than mine. She disagreed.

• I think you know when you're in trouble; you just may not have ways of communicating it. What's acceptable and what isn't depends on your background, the cultural group you're from.

For example, certain kids are from disruptive families. If they have problems, they might fight or break furniture. Someone from, say, an Asian background might become depressed, maybe even suicidal.

• To succeed, you *must* have a sense of your own future. What do you feel is in store for you? You have to feel you're in control, not being controlled.

Don't be rigid when looking at your life and your future. Have goals, and be flexible enough to change them.

• Teenagers often feel that no one understands them. But you *can* find help. You are not alone. People are more alike than different.

16
ANTHONY, 13, AN EIGHTH GRADER

PART I

It hurt in the beginning when people stared at me. I have what's called cerebral palsy, CP. I was born three months premature. I was little. I only weighed about two pounds. Certain of my body functions didn't work right.

I couldn't breath on my own. I was on oxygen for a while. I stayed in the hospital for the first four months of my life before it was okay for my parents to bring me home. Nobody thought I was going to make it. But here I am.

I've always had a positive outlook. My life has taken some turns, but I think that attitude makes the difference. I try not to think, what if I fail at this? Will the surgery work? What if I'm worse?

I try to have faith.

I couldn't walk until I was seven. My legs were too crooked. The most I could do was hold onto my playpen and kind of move on my toes. Then I had surgery on my legs. I had more surgery which was supposed to spread my knees apart.

I still stand with my knees bent and my legs turned out to the side. And I'm still small, the smallest in my class. I was four feet one before this latest surgery. They say after I get the casts off my legs, they'll be straighter. I'll probably be about four feet four.

When I'm not in a wheelchair, the way I am now because I just had this latest surgery, I try to run. I can do that, only not very fast. The way my feet are, I drag them. That slows me down. If the surgery works, my feet will be tilted in, and maybe I'll be able to run just like anybody else.

Some people say, "Oh, poor kid. I feel sorry for you." They try to baby me.

I tell them, "Don't worry about me. If I fall, I fall. I'll get right back up and keep going."

Little kids stare at me the most. I don't get mad at them. They don't know any better. Older adults stare at me, too.

I used to get upset. Now I try to let it go. I am what I am.

There are nights when I feel angry. I wonder, "Why me? What did I do wrong? What did my family do wrong?" I see my older sister doing things and I wonder, "Why me, and not her?" I see kids playing sports. I'm sitting and watching.

Everybody thinks it's going to be someone else's kid who has this problem. But it's got to be somebody, so why *not* me?

God put me on this earth for a purpose. And He put me here the way I am. Maybe He did it for some reason. I don't know. I do know, though, that I can't change who I am.

I think that teenagers have questions they wish they could ask me about CP, but they feel funny doing it. They think I'm going to die from CP. And that's the first thing I tell them.

"I'm going to live to be as old as you are. Maybe older." Some people think I'm totally helpless. Wrong. I'm lucky. I can go places. Do things. A lot of kids with CP are retarded and stuff. I had a light case.

PART II

My sister and my mom are mushy hearts. My sister can hardly stand for them to stick a needle in my arm. I just psych myself that it doesn't hurt. Inside, I worry. The night before any surgery, I think, "What if the doctor

111

makes a mistake?"

Even though I'm just thirteen, I know words that usually only older people do. I know about "checking my vital signs," my heart beat and blood pressure. I know that for surgery they have to strap me on a gurney, like a cot on wheels.

I meet the anesthesiologist — the doctor who gives you the medicine that kind of puts you to sleep. I can tell which doctor has good bedside manners. And I can joke about it with my sister.

She's always taken care of me. I'm thankful for that. We love each other. She's there for me, and I'm there for her.

During my last surgery, I was in the recovery room. The nurse said, "Nobody but parents in here."

My sister walked up to her and said, "What the heck am I? Chopped liver?" She was mad. She had brought balloons for me. Still, like any other brother and sister, we fight. That's normal.

PART III

People with CP can live a normal life. Please don't treat us much different than anybody else. We are like anybody else. Maybe a little less fortunate.

My parents are cool. They don't think I'm helpless. They get on me if I'm lazy, which I am. I admit that. They yell at me the same way they yell at my sister. We get the same punishment.

They are never protective of me, and I'm glad. That's so important to me, to any handicapped kid. I'd be in a mess right now if they'd babied me from the start.

I tell my teachers and my friends, "Don't give me breaks. I don't need pity." When I started junior high last year, my mom wrote my teachers, "Anthony knows his potential." That means I know what I can do and what I can't do.

Some teachers tell me, "Oh, you can't do that." I try it. If I can do it, I go ahead. It's that simple.

Of course, this idea doesn't always work, like, when it comes to girls. I'm interested in them. Some girls say they don't like me — but it's not because of my legs. For some, though, that is the reason.

They're afraid their friends are going to tease them if they like me, someone who's different.

I went to school dances last year. I got up the courage to ask a girl to dance. She said no. I asked someone else. She said no, too.

I ended up dancing with no one but myself.

PART IV

Sometimes I think those of us with troubles are more mature. Rich kids, especially, when they go out into the world won't know what to do. Everything's been handed to them. They won't know about hard work and sacrifice. They won't know about dealing with problems.

I've learned to keep trying and not to quit, even though people may try to get in my way. I know what it's like to go without. To go with pain. To suffer and to still hold on. It's made me stronger. If the world would only treat me like I was normal, I'd be fine.

17
FROM A PERSONALITY-RESEARCH PSYCHOLOGIST

You can use fantasy — your imagination — to bring about positive change in your life.

— Seymour Epstein, Ph.D., professor of psychology, University of Massachusetts; personality-research psychologist, clinical psychologist, author and creator of the concept of constructive thinking, Amherst, Massachusetts

• Anything you can do in real life, you can first do in your mind. You can use fantasy — your imagination — to bring about positive change in your life.

Athletes do this when they train for an event; they visualize it ahead of time in their minds. I learned to type by keeping a copy of the keyboard in my pocket. If I was standing in line with nothing to do, I'd look at it and then move my fingers. I was typing in my imagination.

Let's say you're scared of tests. In your mind, practice and practice taking the exam. Think about what you most fear and learn to make peace with that.

Maybe you're afraid of getting an F. Picture step by step the graded test being passed back. That's the ghost in the closet you don't want to face. That's what your mind is trying to avoid when you *take* the test. That's what produces the anxiety. It could be what makes you not do well.

Then think about what's the *worst* thing that could happen to you if you fail this one test? Yes, you have a problem. There's the F, the evidence of it. Maybe you think, "What an idiot I am. I'll never amount to anything. I might as well quit right now."

But probably you can live with that test result. It's unfortunate, but not a tragedy. You think, "I screwed up. I'd better take a good look at what I did wrong. I can do better."

In other words, you can learn from it, and that's what you're trying to do. You want to get better at it.

This may sound silly, but there's evidence that running things through your imagination first works.

• Let me give you another example. I gained weight. I don't eat much fattening stuff, but

I do like a certain cookie. It's a great cookie. I thought, "How could I use my imagination to change my cookie-eating behavior?"

Cookies are my problem. Your problem might be dieting in general or maybe drugs. So wherever I say "cookie," think about the behavior *you* want to change.

What makes you eat a cookie? It's anticipation, which is imagination. Before you eat it, you have a feeling of how good it will taste.

Now to counter that, think about what happens *after* you eat it. Two minutes later, the cookie's gone, and all you're left with are the consequences. You don't think of that until after you've eaten it.

What if you think of that *before* you eat a cookie and *visualize* it as realistically as you can? Every time you eat a cookie and feel lousy afterward, remember that, so you can recall the feeling.

Okay, you have the cookie in front of you. Imagine you've eaten it. You feel lousy. You know you didn't need it. You were dumb to eat it.

Keep that clear in your mind, and compare it to the joy you get from a half-minute of cookie eating. The anticipation for how good it is gets greatly reduced.

You could also imagine *not* eating the

cookie. You haven't eaten it. How do you feel about yourself? Play it up in your mind. You feel good about sticking to your plan not to eat it. You feel good about making the change you want to make. The desire for the cookie is past, but the good feeling is left.

• How you experience events in your life depends on how you explain them to yourself. There's no hard-and-fast reality. It's what you want to make of it. Let's say somebody insults you. Ask a group of students, "How many of you would be angry?" Almost all raise their hand.

Then you say, "Well, would anyone feel any different?" And maybe one kid says, "I'd be sad."

The other students are shocked. "The guy insulted you!"

And the kid says, "I'm sad that people have so little respect for others that it makes them feel good to hurt others."

Maybe another kid shocks the students even more. "I'd feel sympathetic," she says. "Anybody who goes around insulting people must be troubled. I would try to put him at ease, understand, and help him."

If you do this enough, really think about how else to view events, you can begin to remake who you are in a more positive way.

It's not easy, but it is definitely possible.

• To succeed, change what's called self-talk. Learn to replace your negative, destructive thoughts with constructive thoughts. *And* feel them in your gut!

Think, "I like who I am. I'm a good person. Besides, it's stupid to dislike myself."

Think, "No one's perfect, but I like people."

Think, "When I focus more on the positive than the negative, I feel better, get more done, and people like me better."

Think, "I have a choice between dwelling on my sadness or doing something about it. If I can't change it, at least I can learn something from this bad situation."

18
JENNIFER, 17, A SENIOR

PART I

"Let's go over to John's for a ditching party," I still remember Veronica saying. "There's going to be music and drinks, and maybe weed and cocaine."

I was in ninth grade. Me, Veronica, and Luz, we loved to ditch — to cut school. First, once a week, twice a week, and then the whole week. We got, like, addicted to it. That day, though, I wasn't up for a ditching party.

I went to one a couple days earlier. The guys were all grabbing me, saying, "Do you want to scam?"

In Dallas where I live, scamming means fooling around with a guy you hardly know. You French-kiss and hug. It depends on you, if you want to do sex. When I told him I didn't want to scam *or* get high, he said, "You don't deserve to be with us. You're too stuck up."

No matter what he said, I still liked to have fun, so when Luz said, "Let's go shopping instead," I said, "Why not."

I didn't know that my two so-called friends had plans. What happened was this: In the store after I saw a blouse I liked, Veronica said she'd hold my stuff while I tried it on. She and Luz didn't bother to tell me they were stealing lipstick, perfume, chocolate, and putting it in *my* purse.

So when it came time to leave, they hand it back to me, and all of a sudden, there are bells ringing and a security guard at the door and all these strangers staring at me. I was set up! I couldn't believe it.

"Why did you do this to me?" I screamed.

"What are you talking about, Jennifer?" Luz said. "You know you stole the stuff. You didn't have enough money to pay for it."

A manager grabbed me and started taking things out of my purse. I got scared.

"I swear I didn't do it," I told him.

He said, "I don't believe you. You're a thief."

I couldn't cry. I was too mad at Veronica and Luz. They kept saying I was the one responsible, while again and again I said, *"I didn't do it!"*

Pretty soon, though, they left for home. I was the one caught.

The manager called my mother, even though I begged him to please, please, call my sister. I didn't want to hurt my mom. She was doing everything for me. She didn't deserve this. My heart began to beat hard. "Your mother better hurry up, or we'll take you to jail," the manager said. I remember crying.

When my mother finally got there, at first, I thought she was going to hit me. But worse, she cried, too. That hurt more than if she hit me.

She was suffering, working hard as a single mom to support the family. The manager told her she had to pay $500 to cover the "disruption" I caused!

I felt bad. I also felt nobody could stop me from doing what I wanted to do. Sure, I knew I was hanging around with the wrong people. But right then I wanted to get back at Veronica and Luz. I wanted to tell *their* mothers.

My mom seemed to know that. "Let it go," she said. "For me, for yourself, change. Ask God for his help. He'll take away the pain you feel inside."

I told her, okay; but still it didn't seem fair. Every single day when I went to school, I saw the two of them standing in front of the building, saying how dumb I was. That's painful for a young girl, you know. You wish to defend yourself, but you can't because you are trying to change.

I decided that at least I should be smarter in picking my friends. I'd hang with girls from my neighborhood that I'd known forever. The trouble was, though, that they ditched a lot, too. And I was *so* used to ditching, I didn't know how to stop. On the first nice day, I went back to it like always.

My mom and I fought. She said, "Don't see those girls."

I said, "I love them like sisters. I'd rather be their friend and live with them than live with you."

After a while, my girlfriends got into a gang and said for me to come along. "No," I said, "I'm not going to get beat up for some gang name." Within days, though, two girls from the gang showed up in front of my house. When I said, "Don't try to fight me," one called me a b-i-t-c-h. I was short and thin then. She was big.

The other one said, "I'll kick your ass for sure."

"Okay, if you want to fight me, I'll fight." Right away I hit the one closest to me. She was down, bleeding. I kept on hitting her. I was mad. A gang was nothing for me.

My nineteen-year-old brother came out and told the second girl, "Don't touch my sister. If you get into the fight, I will, too." By then the neighbors were looking. It was awful! *Awful!*

That night I began to think, "What am I doing with my life?" For most of eighth, ninth, and tenth grade, I only cared about having a good time. I didn't once think about success, that I wanted to become somebody. My mind was locked. I didn't want to open it. Even if I did, I didn't have the key.

PART II

Right around then, a counselor, Mr. Seibert, called me to his office. I didn't even know the school had somebody like that since I hardly went, anyway. Actually, everybody considered me a dropout.

He said, "Jennifer, I've been trying to find you for the longest time. Your teachers say that if you come to school, you only stay until second period, and then you leave."

He was right. If you stay until second period, they don't call your home. See, there are a lot of ways to ditch *in* school. Lies you can make up. I should know; I was an expert. I could manipulate people. My reputation was that I was sweet, but had problems.

Over the years, some teachers tried to help me. The thing was I thought they were *old* people. They didn't understand what was going on. In my mind, I couldn't trust them. I didn't believe that anybody could help me. Then.

With Mr. Seibert, in some ways, I think it was timing. I was ready to hear what he said. And, I swear, he made my feelings shake. He looked me square in the eye and said, "I want to understand. I want to know what is going on in your life."

I started to talk. I told him about my friends and the stealing and the gang. I said, "I just wanted to be like them. I wanted them to like me. I wasn't thinking about my future."

"Why don't *you* start planning your life now," he said. "I could help you. I could get you a mentor, a lady to talk to you, to listen to you, to open up new worlds to you." And then he asked about my parents.

"When I was eight years old," I told him, "a drunk driver hit my dad head on. I saw him when he was in the hospital, near death. The doctor was trying to save my dad's life, but I thought she was killing him. I grabbed her and started pushing her away from him.

"I screamed, '*You killed him!*' My mom was there, too. She got on top of his body. I don't know anything more from then. I was in shock."

My dad had been my whole world. I loved him so much, I believed I couldn't live without him. I told my best friend back then, "I don't have anything to live for anymore." After that, there were months that I didn't smile.

I was always asking God, "Why did You do this to me?" One night I even thought I saw my dad in my dream. Alive again. Another time I felt he was there by my bed, touching me. I felt his cold hand. I no longer believed that I deserved to be loved. When my mom asked me, "Why don't you want to talk to me?" I said, "Cause you don't love me."

By the end of the year, we had to sell our beautiful, big house and move into a smaller one in a new neighborhood. I changed schools and lost my friends. My mom went back to teaching. My dad had just a little insurance. We went through most of our savings.

Mr. Seibert brought all that out. He said to me in a quiet voice, "I think your problem is mainly your dad's death. You have to realize that he's gone. He's not coming back. You *have* to go *on* with your life. You have to be a person who is secure, who knows what she wants."

He said my mom loved me. Of course, she did. So did my brother and my sister. They wanted the best for me. He wanted to help me, but I also had to help myself.

"I'm going to talk to your teachers," Mr. Seibert said. "You have to attend night school, too, in order to make up the whole year."

"Okay," I said. And you know what? After I talked to him, I felt better.

The first thing I did was go to my teachers. I had problems, but now I wanted a chance. Would they please give me make-up work? They all said yes.

I had to complete two semesters of serious classes — English, math, stuff like that — in two months! I wouldn't have time for trouble.

For those two months, I would wake up at seven. Get things ready. Go to school. Be in class. Go home. Study. Go to night school. Do that homework. And then sometimes I had to finish the day school work after that! I used to go to sleep at three o'clock in the morning.

By the end of the school year, I didn't make great grades, but I passed. I felt happy *and* tired *and* good about myself. I felt that I could do something. I was worth something.

Everybody was surprised and excited for me, too. My mom, my brother, my sister, Mr. Seibert. I even got known by the principal for what I had done. They knew I was eager.

Sure, then I had to keep it up, but I didn't mind. I went to summer school. And after that in the eleventh grade, there was a new

Jennifer. The first semester, it's hard to believe. I was a 3.8 student in academic classes. The year before my average had been 1.4!

What I was learning, too, was the importance of plans. Without a plan, you fail. But that's not all. It's okay to *change* plans, if you have to, if better opportunities come along.

I saw people that I used to think were nerds. I realized I had been the nerd, not them. They knew what they wanted. I wanted what they had — success. Veronica, Luz, they were gone. They didn't graduate from ninth grade.

I was nominated to take honors classes, not just the regular ones I was in before. I started working with Mr. Seibert as a student counselor, helping other kids with problems similar to mine. They know what they are living, I lived.

When I say, "Life is a headache if you waste your time and don't keep busy," they know I talk from experience.

"Opportunities come," I say. "It's up to you to take them. There is *always* hope and *always* someone to help you. When you feel bad or sad, try to talk to someone. Don't leave things inside. They can only hurt you. Try to let them go. Time, time, time fixes things."

Meanwhile, I studied a lot, and learned a lot. I was responsible. Things were going great for me. I felt secure and like I didn't have any problems.

PART III

Around Thanksgiving, I met Ramon. He was older, already out of school, and worked. He was not a person who had studied that much. But he was funny and sweet and good to me.

To be honest, I have to say, at the beginning, it was a loneliness type of love. I had hardly had any boyfriends. I wanted to know what it felt like — to go with a person seriously, to not feel lonely anymore.

Then after we saw each other for two months, I found out something that depressed me *so* much. Since he respected me — his story — he had another girl to give him what I couldn't. Sex. I felt angry. He'd been lying to me.

"That's it," I told him, once I learned the truth. "We're finished."

A week or two later when he called, I told him, no, I didn't think he deserved another chance. I heard he started drinking a lot.

On Valentine's Day, he showed up drunk in front of my house with his friends. It was raining. He slipped in the mud. Everybody started laughing at him. For a minute I laughed, too. Then I felt sorry for him. As

I helped him up, I said, "You shouldn't come here. I don't want to talk to you."

"But I want to talk to you," he said. "If you won't be my girlfriend or even talk to me anymore, I'm going to move away."

"I don't care," I said, even though I *did* care.

"Okay, but before I leave I want you to have this present," he said, and he gave me a heart-shaped locket. His hand was shaking. Maybe he didn't deserve what I was doing to him. He told me again and again how much he loved me. He wanted me to forgive him.

My tears started coming. I thought to myself, give him another chance.

For a while, things went fine. Ramon was proud I did well in school. I saw him during the week.

On some weekends when he wanted to go out, I didn't always have time for him. I had to study or work or go to a museum or something like that with the lady Mr. Seibert asked to be my mentor. Ramon was jealous. He thought I was doing something else. Not that.

One night I was all dressed up ready to go to school for a special awards ceremony. Ramon was over and said, "Can I kiss you?"

"Not now," I said. "I don't want to mess

my makeup." He grabbed my lipstick and rubbed it all over my face. "This is because you must be going with another guy."

"No, I'm not," I said, "I just want to look presentable. What you did wasn't right."

"I'm going to a party."

He wanted to get me upset, I knew. "Go ahead and leave," I said. "Tonight is important to me. I love you, but I cannot stop my life for you."

PART IV

By then, we seemed to be fighting every day. Mainly, though, we fought about sex. In our culture, Mexican, it's important to be a virgin.

As time went by, and we got to a deeper relationship, Ramon pressured me more. When it finally happened, I cried and said, "Don't ever leave me. What we did means too much to me."

I became obsessed with Ramon, but he wasn't obsessed with me anymore. I told him, "Did you only want me to give up my virginity?"

I bugged him. If he turned his head, I was sure he was looking at another girl. I'd think, he's going to leave me for sure. A week would go by. I wouldn't see him. One time I thought

I was pregnant, and I hadn't heard from him for two weeks!

It was terrible. I had grown used to him being around. I felt depressed and sorry for myself. My grades began to go down.

If I really am pregnant, my life will be over, I thought to myself. Maybe I'm not woman enough to keep somebody's love? Maybe I made a big mistake having sex with him? I should kill myself.

I asked my mom if she would lend me her car. I had to run an errand for school.

I didn't care what happened to me anymore. The speedometer registered fifty miles per hour, as I turned the corner, nearly flipping the car.

At that moment, I swear to you, God put his hand on the wheel. The car stopped with such force I didn't crash. Is God taking care of me? I wondered.

Still, I was hurting inside. Ramon was the only person I loved since my dad. Now I had lost him, too. To me, if I didn't have him, life didn't matter. If I had him, life would be happy.

I forgot he was more interested in me when I was saying no to him than when I was there with my love. I forgot I was changing, and he wasn't. He was drinking again, I heard.

★ ★ ★

I believe in God. That's my main force. It keeps me going. I told my pastor the story of Ramon, how he was the first one. I still loved him; I didn't know what to do. The pastor said, "Leave things up to God."

Ramon stops by and gives me illusions. "See ya tomorrow or the next day," he says, and then three weeks later, a month, he shows up. He's playing with me.

"If you don't love me, tell me," I say.

"I swear I love you." And then he disappears. I'm talking to a wall. Forgetting all my own advice.

"I don't want you with Ramon," my mom says. "Your family and many other people care for you and want you to succeed and be something good."

What am I doing?! It's more than halfway through my senior year. I haven't applied to a single college. I am not going to lose my way over a boyfriend who doesn't deserve my love!

Note: Jennifer applied to four universities and was accepted with full scholarships at all of them. In the fall, she plans to attend Northwestern University, outside of Chicago, Illinois.

19
FROM A COMMUNITY ACTIVIST

It doesn't do any good to be smart if you don't use it.

— *Caryl Ito, M.S.W.; community volunteer; sales and marketing, Bozeman & Associates, San Francisco, California*

• I'm Japanese-American. My parents were in the concentration camps [internment camps] during World War II. My father also served in the U.S. Army. When he came back, I was six months old.

I grew up in Sacramento, California, where there was racial discrimination against the Japanese. My parents were very giving. To help protect us against the prejudice, they raised me and my brother emphasizing that we were proud Japanese.

• In my social work career, I worked with about 2,000 families and children. I saw Hispanic and African-American kids, as well

134

as Asians. I looked at all the issues that seem to stand in the way of people succeeding.

I think that if you know who you are and your family provides you with a kind of inner support, you have a good chance of overcoming any odds against you. If your family isn't able to make you feel secure, then you need outside help.

Take advantage of whatever is positive around you — sports, academics, clubs, whatever. Seek out people who have common values. It only takes two people to support each other.

• It doesn't do any good to be smart if you don't use it!

20
MAX, 15, A SOPHOMORE

PART I

There are still times I wish I could go back to when I'm five years old. I tell my mom what's going on: My stepbrothers are mentally and physically and sexually abusing me. We stop it right then. All these scary things I'm dealing with now — ten years later — are never even part of my life.

I'll begin at the beginning. I live in a respectable little town outside of St. Paul, Minnesota. It's the kind of place where most people don't lock their doors. But they do mind their own business.

Around here you either live in a trailer, on a farm, or — like me — in a house. Until I was five, it was me, my mom, and my dog, Pepper. That was my first dog. She was always there. One time she had puppies in my drawer.

When I was about five and a half, my mom remarried. My stepdad moved in along with his teenage sons. Right away there were fights between his sons and my mom, and me, too. They called me "Mama's Boy" and set about getting me in trouble.

Once the parents left, they said, "Want to be our *best* friend? This is what best friends do. . . ."

They hit me for no reason. They locked me out of the house in my underwear. It was thirty degrees, and the only way to get back in was to break a window. Then I was blamed for it.

Soon, if the parents went out, I begged to stay at the babysitter's. My mom said, "Your stepbrothers will watch you."

"We don't mind," they told her.

My friend down the street, Kenny, saw what happened. "Why do you stay there?" he asked me.

"Where can I go?" I answered. I was too young to stand up for myself.

I turned six, seven, eight.

PART II

One day when I was about nine or ten, I was over at Peter's, a new friend. He was thirteen. His parents put something in their mouths, and then Peter did, too. He said, "It's acid. It'll make you feel better."

The acid took me out of reality and put me

into a dream world. That's where I wanted to be.

Peter's parents were dealers. They didn't see their supply was hit, that we stole drugs from them.

By the time I was eleven, I stopped over there before and after school for acid, grass, coke. During school, I sat there. I wasn't a troublemaker. I was polite. I went through my classes high without my teachers noticing. Since I showed up, they passed me. There was only one counselor who asked me, "What's wrong?"

"I'm going through some difficulties, but I'm okay," I told her.

My stepbrothers had stopped abusing me. My mom had had twins. So she and my stepdad weren't paying attention to me, either. When I came home, if they gave me flak, I clouded it out.

Drugs gave me an I-don't-care attitude. I was so used to being in the dark that I wanted to stay there. I lived behind a wall.

At school, one bully always picked on me. One day he pushed me. When I walked away, he pushed me again. I hit him. Broke his nose. That was the last time he bothered me.

Some of the older guys saw what happened. They let me hang around with them. They treated me like a cool little kid. It felt good for them to say, "Hey, what's up," to me.

I felt comfort. They gave me support. They stuck behind me in everything. They had me be a runner for their drug deals. Later, I dealt.

PART III

Friends tell me I sort of look like a blond Tom Cruise-younger-brother type, whatever. And I've always looked old for my age. By the time I was thirteen, my voice was deep.

Around then I met this girl, Glenda. We spent time together. I told her bits and pieces of my life. But I didn't break down and tell her that I was abused or anything.

Still, there was a bond between Glenda and me. Since she wasn't a big-time drug user, like taking drugs all the time, I slowed down, too.

A couple months later, when she said she was pregnant, I thought, "Great. If I had a kid, I'd have something to call my own."

She couldn't go through with it, she said. Her parents would kill her. She'd have an abortion. But in Minnesota the law says unwed teenagers need their parents' or a judge's permission to get one.

Glenda couldn't stop crying. I didn't know how to cry, so I just tried to give support.

★ ★ ★

The next day I went to school and then to Glenda's. I knocked on her door. No answer. She said she'd be home. I couldn't figure out what was up.

Finally, her mother answered the door. Glenda was dead. Suicide.

PART IV

That did it.

I freak out. I take as much acid and cocaine as I can get my hands on. I am out on the street, hallucinating. I see things crawling all over my body.

I crash my beer bottle up against the wall and stick it into my leg. I am bleeding, but I don't realize it. The next thing I know, I'm in a hospital with an IV in my arm.

The parents are there. They are concerned, and angry. "You're ruining our reputation," they tell me.

When I come back home, I feel dead inside. I do the only thing I know how to do. Drugs. Later on, my stepdad asks me to clean my room. I say, no. He reaches back and hits me. I pull out my knife and tell him to get away.

By morning, they kick me out of the house and send me to an aunt and uncle's.

I like those relatives. They respect me. But

pretty soon I'm out of drugs, and there, I don't have connections. I panic.

I tell my aunt I'm going for a walk. But something inside me tells me, *I need help.*

I go to this guy's house, some stranger, and take his motorcycle. I drive it down the street to a parking lot and then back to his driveway. The cops notice. They take me down to the station.

I have no drug record. I brought the bike back. It's a practical joke, they think. "You're free to go."

I start to leave. I stop. I hear myself screaming, *"I can't go back on the street. I'm too hooked up with drugs and my life is just f—king up!"*

A police captain decides I'm a danger to myself. "Get a case worker."

"I'd suggest therapy," she says.

PART V

I am walking through pain. I don't care *where* I am. I have a problem; what I don't know is, can I face it?

Every day for months I want to kill myself. I make myself think of reasons not to. I don't want to make others suffer. I like to make people laugh.

I start to draw, small pencil drawings of futuristic things. I am proud of them. I work out. Twice a week I go to group therapy. I talk. I cry.

My mom and stepdad agree to go to a few therapy sessions with me. When I say, "I was abused," my stepdad yells, "I don't believe you!"

I call my stepbrothers. "Why did you do that to me when I was a kid?" They say my mom caused their parents' divorce. They wanted to get back at her. They didn't know it would bother me.

At school, I'm put in a special class. The teacher's strict. We can't swear, fight, or put people down.

We learn to solve problems and make decisions. If I have a problem, I write down what led up to it. How I feel about it. And what I can do about it. Then I list all the ways of solving the problem and choose the best one.

It's been a year and a half since Glenda's death. I'm straight now. Except I smoke. I have a B average. Inside, I'm stronger. Like, this morning I was on the edge. Later on, I got in an argument with a friend. Tonight I had a lousy conversation with my mom.

I said to myself "How do I deal with this? And what are the consequences of each of those actions?"

If I deal with what's bothering me, I feel better. If I ignore it, I feel bad.

For the first time maybe ever, I have goals. I was asked to help with a program for abused kids. I've "adopted" two little brothers. They're both shy.

I tell them, "Don't let others get to you. Someday you'll be somebody. Other people will like you. People who put you down are jealous. They envy you."

I get together with them on Tuesdays. They have my number if they want to talk. I've grown to love those little boys.

Note: I call Max back two months later. How is he, I want to know. "He's gone," his teacher says. "His parents put him in a group home. He wanted to stay with them. They said, 'No,' so he took off.

"I hope he makes it; that this is just a temporary setback," the teacher adds. "He has a good head on his shoulders. The question is, how will he make money? Prostitution? Drugs? At fifteen, can he find work that's legal? That brings in enough to support him?"

21
FROM A MAYOR

Seek advice.

— *Mary Chapar Moran, Mayor,*
Bridgeport, Connecticut

• My parents were immigrants from a village
in Syria. Even though I was born in the United
States, I didn't speak English until I was five.
We played our childhood games in Arabic.

At home we were taught four basic loves:
love of God, love of family, love of country,
and love of one another.

What I tell my own kids, I tell you. Whatever spiritual being you pray to, make that
the center of your life. Live by those stan-
dards.

• After that, to succeed in your own personal
quest, seek advice. Do the best you can at
what you do. It doesn't matter what job you
have. Do it well. Go out there with pride.

• Don't be afraid to make mistakes; you learn

from them. But try to make them your *own* mistakes. Be your own person. And in your quest, no matter what problems you have, if you try to help others, you'll get a lot of satisfaction. It will motivate you to be a better person.

• We live in a country where you can be anything you want. But you have to work hard. You have to *sacrifice* to get there. I'm proof positive it can be done.

Without a college degree, I run a city with a 300 million-dollar budget and 4,000 employees. I pray all the time for strength and guidance, and it's working. It can with you, too.

22

MATTHEW, 19, A COLLEGE FRESHMAN

PART I

Someday I want to write a book. I'll call it *No Longer Silent*. I'll write about life with no father. The guys in my Oakland neighborhood. The night of the fight, and the jail for kids.

I'll write about San Quentin too, the maximum security prison. I came there when I was sixteen. I was one of the youngest guys then. When I left four months ago, there were lots of guys that age.

Some of them were going crazy, cutting each other with razors, extorting, raping, taking drugs. I was *always* scared.

I used to wake up at night and look at the wall of my cell. I'd see a black face with tears dropping down from the eyes. Behind him were the drug pushers, the killers, the pimps, the ghetto. He didn't know what he wanted out of life.

"Never again," I say to myself now. I will

never go back to prison. I will make whatever sacrifices necessary. If it means going to school, I'll do it. If it means not hanging out with the guys, I'll do it.

If it means getting a low-paying job for nothing more than the hope I can take that experience and invest it later in something that will prosper, I'll do it.

What makes one person succeed and not another is a willingness to make sacrifices.

PART II

I never knew my father. He left my mother when I was a few months old. She never got over it. I don't think I did, either. Sometimes I say, "If my father had been there, he would have guided me. . . ."

Growing up, kids need a role model, someone to look up to. Where I live, there aren't many positive ones. The people who get respect are active.

People talk about them. They have the girls. They're into fun and parties. They're the hoodlums, and I thought they were interesting.

But still my mother tried to make things right. She's a hardworking lady. She's worked at dry cleaners, grocery stores, offices, wherever.

The summer I was fourteen, I worked at

a doughnut store. One day I had an argument with a rude customer. The boss told me, "Cool down. Take the night off."

I got on my bike and never came back.

My mother didn't want me to be someplace where I was uncomfortable. So when I quit my job, she looked at me and said, "Oh, well."

It's sad. Kids make big decisions, and we don't know how they are going to affect our lives. I didn't. I was just thinking about hanging out with the guys.

I wanted to be one of the guys. I didn't want to be one of those doing the wrong things. But I wanted to be around them. It gave me security and respect if others knew I was with them. And that was important in my neighborhood. You don't get much respect for being a bookworm.

At first, we weren't looking for trouble. Later, though, we got guns. We shot them sometimes, like at block parties. Then we got involved in drugs.

PART III

Have you ever been in an automobile accident? Everything is going the way it's supposed to. Then out of nowhere, a crash happens. Your world is upside down. That's the way I felt about the fight.

My friend and a guy from the other group had an argument about drugs or a girl. I was just there.

Suddenly, I didn't know what the hell was happening. Were these guys surrounding me? Or was it just my imagination?

It was a frenzy.

A guy gave me a knife. I didn't even know him. I'd met him a couple weeks ago. He came out of nowhere. Then he disappeared. I was scared.

I was confused. I ran through . . . I stabbed someone. I didn't know for sure. I didn't mean to.

I'd never stabbed anybody before. I dropped the knife and ran home.

The next thing I heard, somebody had got stabbed and died. He was nineteen.

"Turn yourself in," my family said. "It's the best thing to do."

I couldn't believe it. I was fourteen years old and charged with murder. One minute everything was fun and games. Then life was serious. I wanted to close my eyes and wake up with everything back to normal.

Instead, I went to the police station. I stood in a lineup. Someone picked me out. I went to court and was put in the jail for kids. The

Youth Authority.

Most of the guys were my age — fourteen, fifteen, and sixteen. Some had done worse crimes than me. I was no angel, but I wasn't made for prison, either. It was a different society from the outside.

You wear a uniform. A monkey suit, we called it. There was a schedule: up at six, three squares — meals — a day, school, and at ten o'clock, lights out.

The officers don't treat you like a person. They push you. They hit you. They put you down in front of the others. You feel inferior. That pain is the worst.

Most kids in jail are fascinated by the people in "Q," San Quentin, maximum security. They seem to want to get farther into the system. Into the lifestyle. These kids are wild. Hostile. Angry. They don't know what they want or what to do with their time.

New people come in; they want to test you. The law is do whatever you have to do to survive. And often to survive you have to do what the other guys do, even if you don't want to.

I tried to stay low-key.

My mother came to visit me. She cried. I hurt everybody in my family. I felt dead inside. Prison took my world away. I would never see trees again. I hated every bit of it.

PART IV

Looking back, I wish I got stiffer time. It would have helped me more. After months of going back and forth to court, I pleaded guilty. I got probation. I was out.

I went back to school. I focused. I did okay. It gave me confidence that I could compete. But at the same time I had this misconception: I didn't have to let my past life go. I thought I could go to school, please my probation officer, and *still* hang out with the guys.

These were my friends. Regular guys I'd known forever. These weren't the ones on the corner. They went to school. They had good families.

I loved these guys. I trusted them. We had fun together. We stood for each other. If one of us had a fight or needed the others, we were there. They meant the world to me.

One of them, though, messed with the wrong crowd. They killed him. I knew him for years. It knocked us right in the head.

We knew who the guys were. And they declared war on us all. They came to my school, to look for me. I got scared. As much as I wanted to be part of an academic world, I was still part of the guys.

I knew I was on probation. But, I thought, if I don't arm myself, I'll be dead.

I gave up on the idea of being successful. I conformed to my environment. I got a gun. When this guy confronted me, I shot him. Wounded him.

The police came. At sixteen, I felt defeated. I thought, I won't make it to seventeen.

I wasn't sent to the jail for kids. This was no joke. This was San Quentin.

After being sentenced, I hurt bad. I had no more chances. I was going into an unknown world and I looked so young. I *was* young. Would I stand up to the pressures?

They locked me in a cell for twenty-three hours a day. By myself. It's that way for everybody — your reception — while you're being classified. For me, it lasted three months.

To survive, I read. I read W.E.B. DuBois, Martin Luther King Jr., civil rights books, the Bible, the Koran. I read every newspaper I could get my hands on.

To overcome the enemy, whether it's drugs, crime, or poverty, I had to know the news.

I had the desire to *change*. I said to myself, "To hell with this, man. I'm going to be my own person!"

I made a clear decision to stop the life I

was living. I might have done some stupid things, but I never lost touch that I could be better. I hoped it wasn't too late.

Within a month, I got my GED. I wish I tried to do that before.

PART V

In "Q" I was no longer with people my age. I was with guys thirty, forty, fifty. Some of the old-timers liked me. They thought of me like a little brother.

Others, though, looked at me as being something else to them. I had to be careful. I didn't want to be fair play.

Some guys come there, they're home. For me, it was painful. I used to always think, think, think.

What could I do to make my life different? What could I do when I came home? I tried to think of a *plan*. I wanted to say, "This is the way."

Later I realized I should have *alternatives*. Be flexible. I didn't know how society would accept me once I got out. Some people do. Others close all doors. I had to be ready for both ways.

A lot of people have never been taught to think. They're taught to cope. I wanted to help myself and others, too.

I became involved in an inmate-run group. It was a cultural awareness program. Most of the staff was white; most of the inmates, black and Hispanic. Part of the purpose of this group was to ease race tensions.

As the time went by, I ran into guys I'd known in the streets. People close to me. They were still looking for the ghetto to continue the vicious cycle. I wanted to make the ghetto a better place. I was in search of peace and tranquility.

I told them, "Man, join this organization." They only thought about the next visit from their girl. I didn't want to be with them. I was changing. I was making progress.

I gave *myself* a pat on the back for this success. Also I knew success was *not* about money. It was *not* about getting respect by having an iron hand and a backup.

I told my family, "Don't come visit. Let me feel the pain." In a way I was scared to go home. Go back to society. I was afraid of what the future held for me. I feared the unknown.

I got depressed. I just turned eighteen. I had accomplished nothing. Most sixteen-, seventeen-, eighteen-year-olds were enjoying life, going to school. I was inside a penitentiary with men three times my age.

It gave me a realistic perspective on life. On time.

Five or six guys inside helped me. Maybe it was me in search of a father. Interesting. I never thought about that until today. I trusted them. They encouraged me.

They'd say, "Are you going to get out and do the same thing again?"

"No," I'd say. "I don't need to now."

I learned an important lesson from them. If you have some people, some adults, who're willing to help you, *let them help you.* The guys on the corner ain't going to be there for you. When you need that shoulder, they'll have disappeared.

An older inmate told me he was in jail on a robbery charge since 1982. He said, "Lots of folks take time for granted. We misuse it. Time becomes our enemy and passes us by."

I listened.

I became time-conscious and death-conscious. "A person who is conscious of death is unlikely to disregard time," he said. "You know it's going to run out one day."

He reminded me that I'm only human. There's a higher force.

I thought about the guy who died because of me. I have never forgiven myself for that. Even to this day, I still think about it. The pain I caused his family. How can I mend that?

It was never my intent to kill somebody. I deeply regret it. All I wanted to do was have fun.

I lost focus. I almost lost what I wanted to do with my life. In a way, though, his death inspired me to go on, at the times when I thought the pressure was unbearable.

I went into prison a little kid; I left there a man. I had pre-planned what I was going to do once I got out. I knew I would start college. I applied and was accepted when I was still inside.

The semester started January 25. I thought I would get out earlier, but the parole board had the dates screwed. I became discouraged. I was doing all I could to make myself successful and change. They were throwing a wrench in my engine.

I was frightened. I didn't want to fall out of focus. I didn't want to start hanging out and selling drugs and doing all those mother-f——r things. I told myself, "Reach out for help." I called home, and they called people in Oakland.

Finally, I got released on a Monday. By dinner, I was home, and I left my house the next morning at 7:00 A.M. for classes. I only missed the first week. It didn't matter.

I had mentally prepared myself for that day, for that transition. I knew what I had to do and how I had to do it . . . to make it. And I did okay in school — all B's. I'm going to do better this semester.

I also realize that because I just had my nineteenth birthday, I'm about the age of most freshmen. There is no way to tell that I have been separated from society. I'm right back in there, competing, accomplishing things.

It shows, I think, if you really try to be somebody and put work into it, you can make it.

I love America. But one thing disturbs me. It's good to be an individual. Still, we should understand that we have a commitment to our community as well. It's not all about me, me, me being successful. It's about making things better. That's *my* passion.

I only hope that you kids who read this book *think* about life and time. As long as you're living, each day becomes a chance to do better than you did yesterday.

You're not guaranteed anything in this world but to die. Don't limit yourself. Do all that you can do to make the best of the life you've been given.

23
THE BEGINNING

The voice in your head may say, "I feel dead inside. What I'm doing is wrong. I'm better than this."

But even if you want to trade failure for success, you wonder, how exactly do you start?

I ask the adults, "Why *do* certain people succeed more than others?"

Silence.

Then some of them half-jokingly answer, "Let me know what you find out."

I go through my notes and my tapes a final time. After taking notes from my notes, I come to these conclusions.

The first step to success is to make the decision. You don't want to keep living the way you are. You want to turn your life around.

Then, for your map of this journey, for support, and for key ideas of how to do it, re-read the stories of teens overcoming problems similar to yours. Let them serve as your guides and as your reminders.

You are not alone.

These kids all know the road to success *isn't* easy. Along the way, you get depressed. You feel discouraged. You mess up. You want to quit. But then, you try again.

Those who don't give up, who are succeeding, seem to share certain characteristics. I made a list of them below.

Read each sentence carefully. Make a copy for yourself. Take these words seriously. Understand that they've worked for others.

You'll recognize these things. They are not mysterious or magical. Maybe, though, they will help you, too. They're a beginning.

Reach out for help — to a parent, a neighbor, a teacher, a preacher, a coach, or a counselor. There is nothing wrong with asking adults for guidance. Then, listen to them.

Help others. Be there for your friends, for your neighbors, for younger kids — offer the same good advice you have discovered yourself.

Have a belief in yourself that is stronger than anyone's disbelief in you.

Keep so busy you don't have time for trouble:

keep up with your schoolwork, hold a job, do volunteer work, participate in school or community projects.

Don't be afraid of new ideas, new people, and new cultures.

Believe in the future. Make today's decisions part of your planning for the long haul. Evaluate ahead of time the results of your actions. It's okay to change your mind.

Read a lot — for information, for fun, for escape.

Don't generalize based on a single event. Flunking one test doesn't mean you're a failure for life. Instead, it reminds you to study harder next time.

Believe in a higher spiritual force and a moral code.

Feel good about yourself. See events around you in an optimistic, positive way. Don't let life overwhelm you.

Keep trying to succeed. Think of yourself as patient, yet determined. Success comes in small steps. There's always a way.

Give yourself pep talks: Push yourself not to give up. Praise yourself when you succeed.

Have friends, but be true to your heart. Don't be influenced by group decisions you know are wrong.

Want to succeed, to be somebody, to be proud of who you are and where you are heading.

FOR FURTHER READING

Argyle, Michael. *The Psychology of Happiness.* New York: Methuen, 1987.

Baldwin, Christina. *One to One: Self-Understanding Through Journal Writing.* New York: M. Evans, 1977.

Booher, Dianna Daniels. *Making Friends With Yourself and Other Strangers.* New York: Julian Messner, 1982.

Branden, Nathaniel. *How to Raise Your Self-Esteem.* New York: Bantam Books, 1987.

Briggs, Dorothy Corkille. *Celebrate Yourself.* Garden City, New York: Anchor Press/ Doubleday, 1986.

Corson, John. *Stress, Self-Concept and Violence.* New York: AMS Press, 1989.

Csikszentmihalyi, Mihaly, and Reed Larson. *Being Adolescent: Conflict and Growth in the Teenage Years.* New York: Basic Books, Inc., 1984.

Elkins, Dov Peretz, ed. *Self-Concept Sourcebook: Ideas and Activities for Building Self-Esteem.* Rochester, New York: Growth Assoc., 1979.

Epstein, Alice. *Mind, Fantasy, and Healing.* New York: Delacorte, 1989.

Gray, Mattie Evans. *Images: A Workbook for Enhancing Self-Esteem and Promoting Career Preparation, Especially for Black Girls.* Sacramento, California: California State Department of Education, 1988.

Helmstettler, Shad. *The Self-Talk Solution.* New York: William Morrow, 1987.

Johnson, John H., with Lerone Bennett, Jr. *Succeeding Against the Odds.* New York: Warner, 1989.

Kassorla, Irene. *Go for It!* New York: Dell Publishing Co., Inc., 1984.

Lanker, Brian. *I Dream a World: Portraits of Black Women Who Changed America.* New York: Stewart, Tabori & Chang, 1989.

McFarland, Rhoda. *Coping With Stigma.* New York: The Rosen Publishing Group, 1989.

————. *Coping Through Self-Esteem.* New York: The Rosen Publishing Group, 1988.

Maehr, Martin, and Larry Braskamp. *The Motivation Factor: A Theory of Personal Investment.* Lexington, Massachusetts: Lexington Books, 1986.

Meyer, Donald. *The Positive Thinkers: Popular Religious Psychology from Mary Baker Eddy to Norman Vincent Peale and Ronald Reagan.* Middletown, Connecticut: Wesleyan University Press, 1988.

Newman, Robert. *Reading, Writing and Self-esteem.* Englewood Cliffs, New Jersey: Prentice-Hall, 1982.

Peale, Norman Vincent. *The Positive Principle Today: How to Renew and Sustain the Power of Positive Thinking.* Englewood Cliffs, New Jersey: Prentice-Hall, 1976.

Reynolds, Barbara. *And Still We Rise.* Washington, D.C.: USA Today Books, 1988.

Sanford, Linda Tschirhart, and Mary Ellen Donovan. *Women and Self-Esteem: Understanding and Improving the Way We Think and Feel About Ourselves.* Garden City,

New York: Anchor Press/Doubleday, 1984.

Shames, Laurence. *The Hunger for More: Searching for Values in An Age of Greed.* New York: Times Books, Inc., 1989.

Steinhart, Lawrence. *The Crucial Questions: A New Age Approach to Self-Discovery.* Norfolk, Virginia: Donning Co., 1989.

T, Mr., with Peter Elbling. *Be Somebody (Or Be Somebody's Fool).* New York: St. Martin's Press, 1984.

Vedral, Joyce. *I Can't Take it Anymore: How to Get Up When You're Really Low.* New York: Ballantine Books, 1987.

Wesson, Carolyn McLenahan. *Teen Troubles: How to Keep Them From Becoming Tragedies.* New York: Walker & Company, 1988.

The employees of THORNDIKE PRESS hope you have enjoyed this Large Print book. All our Large Print books are designed for easy reading — and they're made to last.

Other Thorndike Large Print books are available at your library, through selected bookstores, or directly from us. Suggestions for books you would like to see in Large Print are always welcome.

For more information about current and upcoming titles, please call or mail your name and address to:

THORNDIKE PRESS
PO Box 159
Thorndike, Maine 04986
800/223-6121
207/948-2962